Janice VanCleave's Physics for Every Kid

Easy Activities That Make Learning Science Fun

Janice VanCleave

Second Edition

JB JOSSEY-BASS™

A Wiley Brand

Illustrations by Tina Cash Walsh.

Jossey-Bass

A Wiley Imprint 111 River St, Hoboken, NJ 07030 www.josseybass.com

Jossey-Bass books and products are available through most bookstores. To contact Jossey-Bass directly, call our Customer Care Department within the U.S. at 800–956–7739, outside the U.S. at +1 317 572 3986, or fax +1 317 572 4002.

Wiley also publishes its books in a variety of electronic formats and by print-on-demand. Some material included with standard print versions of this book may not be included in e-books or in print-on-demand. If this book refers to media such as a CD or DVD that is not included in the version you purchased, you may download this material at http://booksupport.wiley.com. For more information about Wiley products, visit www.wiley.com.

Library of Congress Cataloging-in-Publication Data

ISBN 9781119654285 (paperback), 9781119654315 (ebook), 9781119654292 (ebook)

Cover illustrations by Tina Cash Walsh
Cover design by Paul McCarthy

Printed in the United States of America

SECOND EDITION

SKY10026555_042621

Table of Contents

Introduction

Throughout the writing of this book, I have daydreamed about the fun I have teaching hands-on physics. I've pictured children and educators enjoying these science activities, while reading instructions that are clear and easy to follow and simple explanations about what happened and why. Science safety was a primary concern when designing the activities in this book. It is my fervent hope that this physics book will ignite a profound curiosity for scientific discovery in readers of all ages. The bottom line is that I want to share my passion for physics and how exciting and relevant science is to our everyday lives.

One doesn't need a degree in science to benefit from learning more about why magnets stick to the fridge door and not to a wooden door. Wonder how a parachute works? Why does a magnifying glass make things look bigger? I imagine children of all ages stopping and questioning the physical world around us. Scientific investigations help develop patterns and higher-level thinking to solve real, everyday problems.

The order of presentation is designed to provide a physics foundation upon which to build new principles of science. The activities in each specific topic spiral in content.

Throughout the activities, certain words and phrases are in bold; the meanings of these are given in the Glossary at the end of the book. Working through the activities in order is suggested. However, any activity has educational value on its own merit. With the help of the Glossary, as well as introductions for various topics, you can pick and choose any investigation and be rewarded with a successful experiment. Of course, a good outcome depends upon following the procedure steps in order. Substituting equipment can affect the results for some activities, but science is meant to be fun so trust your judgment about changes.

This book was designed to give the reader a taste of physics:

Energy Learn about stored energy, energy of moving objects and the transfer between them, and the study of different forms of energy including mechanical, electrical, sound, and light. Energy is simply the ability to do work, which means to change or deform or move an object, and to create heat.

Force and Motion Learn about the effect of forces acting on an object, and study about the force of gravity and how it affects falling objects. A study of Sir Isaac Newton's Three Laws of Motion and how they apply to our everyday lives is covered.

Simple Machines Learn about simple machines which are mechanical devices that change the direction and/or magnitude (size) of a force. Levers, inclined planes, wedges, wheels and axles, pulleys, and screws are studied.

Magnets Learn about magnets and their effect, including an invisible field around magnets responsible for the most remarkable property of a magnet, which is a force that pulls on other magnetic materials, such as iron, and attracts or repels other magnets.

The Activities

This book is written to guide you through the steps necessary in successfully completing a science experiment and to present methods of solving problems and making discoveries.

Introduction: Background information provides knowledge about the topic of the investigation and generally describes cause and effect relationships that you can investigate.

See for Yourself: A list of common but necessary materials and step-by-step instructions on how to perform the experiment is provided.

What Happened? A statement of the predicted outcome is provided with a discussion of what should have happened during the activity. A scientific explanation of what was observed is provided using understandable language and technical, scientific vocabulary so that readers of any age can master the scientific principles involved and discuss their findings.

General Instructions

1. **Read first.** Read each experiment completely before starting.
2. **Collect needed supplies.** You will experience less frustration and more fun if all the necessary materials for the experiments are ready and set up for easy access.
3. **Experiment.** Follow each step very carefully, never skip steps, and do not add your own. Safety is of the utmost importance. By reading the experiment before starting, you will be able to note any safety warnings. Then, follow

instructions exactly so you can feel confident that your outcome will have the desired results.

4. **Observe.** If your results are not the same as described in the experiment, carefully reread the instructions, and start over from the beginning. Check to make sure your materials are as described and in good working order. Use the illustrations to see if the activity is set up properly. Consider factors, such as the ambient temperature, humidity, lighting, and so on, that might affect the results.

Measurements

Measuring quantities described in this book are given in imperial units followed by approximate metric equivalents in parentheses. Unless specifically noted, the quantities listed are not critical, and a variation of a very small amount more or less will not alter the results.

Foreword

Imagine a toddler gleefully dropping a bottle off the high-chair tray. Their parent returns the bottle to its rightful place only to see it dropped again. And each time the bottle falls to the floor. This toddler and Sir Isaac Newton have something in common. They both find physics delightful! Janice VanCleave knows that this toddler is learning about the laws of physics! This book is written for every kid who wants to keep dropping things, rolling things, and, most of all, wants to keep learning about the physical world.

And who hasn't wondered about how something as large as an airplane can stay up in the sky? Janice VanCleave never wants that sense of wonder to end. Written for people of all ages with a curiosity about the world around us, this book will be a treasure for the homeschooling parent or classroom teacher that wants to add easy-to-do science that promises to have kids asking, "Is it time for science yet?"

Each activity starts out with a clear explanation of a scientific phenomenon. We have all played with magnets. But did you know that you can map an invisible magnetic force field with a compass? Soon, you find yourself eagerly gathering a few common household materials because the activity is so enticing you can't wait to try it! Each science activity, often deceptively simple, is followed by an explanation that uses everyday language to explain complex principles. It is simply astounding to experiment with something that you have seen a million times, but for the first time you really understand the science. Wow.

Janice VanCleave is a teacher at heart. Her true passion is explaining science in a way that anyone can understand it. This book is a treasure. It unlocks the mystery of physical laws that we see every moment of every day.

I can't help but think that one day the baby who dropped the bottle off the highchair tray will open this book. Then, a true adventure of science discovery and learning will take place. Once again, exploring physics will be delightful! Perhaps that kid will grow up to be the first person to walk on Mars. Anything is possible.

Mary Bowen

I
Energy Introduction

Energy is the capacity to do work. In **physics**, work is done when a force is applied to an object causing it to move. A **force** is a pushing or pulling action on an object. Forces are measured in pounds (lb) or **newtons** (N), where 1 lb = 4.5 N. **Work** occurs only when a force causes something to move. If you push on a tree and it doesn't move, then no work has been done even though the effort may have exhausted you. Study how work is calculated in this important equation: $W = F \times d$; where W is the work done; F is a specific force and d is the distance moved. Comparatively, when the equation is $W = F_{net} \times d$, the work being done considers all forces (F_{net}) that are acting on the object that is being moved, including frictional forces. **Weight** is a measure of Earth's gravitational force pulling an object down toward the center of Earth. Gravity is the force of **attraction** between two objects with mass. Yes, your body has a force of attraction on other objects, but it is such a minute force that it is basically ineffective. Whereas, the mass of Earth is great enough to produce a force that pulls things on or near Earth's surface down. Down means toward the center of Earth; thus, when you drop something, it falls perpendicular to Earth's surface. Forces do not always cause **linear motion**, which is motion in a straight line. **Torque** is a turning force that causes motion around a center point, such as the turning of a lid or the spinning of a merry-go-round.

Movement is the change of an object's physical position. Linear movement is measured in feet (ft) or centimeters (cm), where 1 ft = 30 cm. Not all movement is linear or rotational but rather some objects **vibrate**, meaning they move back and forth. **Frequency** is a measure of the number of times something happens in a specific amount of time. Frequency can be measured in **hertz** (**Hz**), where 1 Hz = 1 cycle per second or one back and forth vibration.

Potential energy is the energy an object has because of its position relative to some zero position. It is energy that has the potential to do 'work.' Two types of potential energy investigated in this book are **gravitational potential energy** and **elastic potential energy.**

Gravitational potential energy is the stored energy an object has because of its position above a specific ground zero. This type of potential energy is due to the force of gravity acting on the object. To obtain this energy, work had to be done on an object to raise it to a higher level above ground zero, such as placing a book on a top shelf with the floor below being ground zero. Gravitational potential energy is directly related to the mass of the object as well as its height above ground zero. When the book is dropped from a specific height, its gravitational potential energy is converted to kinetic energy as the book falls.

Elastic potential energy is the energy stored in an object that can be stretched or compressed. A force is needed to compress or stretch an elastic object. Consider a trampoline, which has the greatest elastic potential energy

2

when it is stretched the most, as does a rubber band. A coiled spring stores elastic potential energy when a force compresses it as well as when a force stretches it. In both cases, when the spring is released, the spring's elastic potential energy results in the wound coils moving back to their normal position. Thus, the elastic potential energy is converted to kinetic energy.

Kinetic energy (KE) is the energy of objects that are moving. Remember, kinetic energy does not cause an object to move, instead objects have kinetic energy because they are moving. A ball at the top of a ramp has gravitational potential energy. As the ball rolls down the ramp, its gravitational potential energy is converted to kinetic energy. There are three types of kinetic energy: vibrational, rotational, and translational. **Vibrational KE** is the energy caused by a back and forth movement; **rotational KE** is the result of turning about an axis, and **translational KE** is the result of linear movement from one place to another.

Mechanical energy is the sum of an object's potential energy and kinetic energy. Objects have mechanical energy if they are moving or have positional potential energy. Remember that an object doesn't have to be a machine to have mechanical energy. For example, both rivers and wind have mechanical energy.

In addition to mechanical energy activities, other types of energy will be investigated: sound energy, electrical energy, and light energy.

Sound is the sensation perceived by an organism's sense of hearing produced by the stimulation of hearing organs by sound **waves**. **Sound energy** is a type of energy produced by vibrating objects, such as when a guitar string is plucked. The movement of the string moves the air

3

around it, producing a pattern of disturbances in the air called sound waves. Sound energy is transferred through mediums, such as solids, liquids, and gases. This type of energy can be heard by humans and other animals.

Electricity is a type of energy that we often take for granted until it is not available. All electric appliances, including computers and TVs do not work if the electric power line bringing electrical energy to your home is broken during a storm. You will discover more about **current electricity** as well as how to perform magic tricks using **static electricity** in the activities included in this book. You will also learn how the chemical energy stored in batteries produces the current electricity necessary for cell phones and tablets. Other electrical terms such as **free electrons**, **conductors**, **insulators**, **polarization**, and **closed** and **open circuits** will be investigated in the activities related to electrical energy.

Light energy is radiation. **Radiation** is a type of wave energy that does not need a medium to move through, such as radiation from the Sun that moves through space to Earth. The term radiation can sound dangerous and frightening, but did you know that common visible light and heat waves, called infrared light, are all forms of radiation? We can't imagine homes without our useful microwave oven. There are seven types of radiation: gamma rays, X-rays, ultraviolet light, visible light, infrared light, microwaves, and radiowaves.

1. Energy Conservation

The Law of Conservation of Energy states that energy is neither created nor destroyed. Instead, energy can be converted, or changed, into another form of energy. In this activity, the mechanical energy of a pendulum will be investigated. **Mechanical energy** is the summation of an object's **potential energy** (stored energy) and **kinetic energy** (energy of moving objects). A **pendulum** is a weight, called a **bob**, hung from a fixed point so that it can freely move backward and forward. Each swing of the bob, from one side to the other forms an arc, as shown in Figure 1. Work is done on the pendulum when it is raised to position A. This means that energy is being transferred to the pendulum. When raised, the pendulum gains **gravitational potential energy**, which is stored energy due to an object's height. When released, gravity pulls the pendulum down and its gravitational potential energy is converted into kinetic energy.

Gravity is the force of attraction between any two objects with mass in the Universe. The greater the mass, the greater is an object's gravitational force. Earth is very massive; thus, it attracts objects near or on its surface in a direction toward its center. At position A, the pendulum has maximum gravitational potential energy, which is changed to kinetic energy as the pendulum swings down to position B. From position B to C, the pendulum is moving against the downward force of gravity; thus, it slows. During this upward part of the swing, the pendulum's kinetic energy changes into gravitational potential energy again.

C   A

B

FIG 1

The mechanical energy of a pendulum involves the transfer of kinetic energy into potential energy and back to kinetic energy, and so on. It is important to note that the amount of potential energy at position C is less than it was when the pendulum was first lifted to position A (Figure 1). This means the pendulum loses mechanical energy with each swing and each swing is lower and lower until it finally stops. This lost energy was changed into another form of energy, such as heat or sound (air vibration).

See for Yourself

Materials

string, 8 inch (20 cm)

tape

washer with a hole or any comparable weight

What to Do

1. Tie one end of the string to the washer.
2. Tape the free end of the string to the edge of a table (Figure 2).

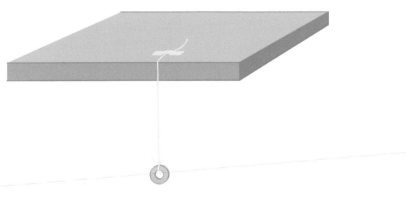

FIG 2

3. Pull the pendulum to the side a short distance and release. It should swing back and forth. Observe the movement of the pendulum. Make note of the pendulum's height during each swing.

7

What Happened?

In Figure 1 the pendulum is first held stationary at position A, which is higher than position C. This means work has been done on the pendulum by lifting it, giving the pendulum gravitational potential energy. When the pendulum is released, the force of gravity acts on the pendulum pulling it downward. When moving, the pendulum has kinetic energy. Halfway between A and B, half of the mechanical energy is divided between potential energy and kinetic energy. At position B, the potential energy of the pendulum is zero and the kinetic energy is at its maximum. This kinetic energy decreases as the pendulum moves toward position C. Halfway between B and C, mechanical energy is again divided between potential energy and kinetic energy. Finally, the pendulum rises slightly below position C. In this position, its potential energy is less than at the start of the swing. This reduction of mechanical energy decreases incrementally until the pendulum stops moving and hangs vertically at a standstill at position B.

2. Frequency

Frequency is how many times an event occurs in a specific amount of time, such as the back and forth swing of a pendulum. A pendulum is an apparatus with a hanging weight from a fixed point that can move freely back and forth. A string with a washer attached to the end is one example of a pendulum. The weight on a pendulum is called the bob. Each forward and back swing of the bob on a pendulum is counted as one cycle.

The frequency of a pendulum is determined by counting the number of cycles, the back and forth movements, the pendulum bob makes in a one-second interval. The length of the cable or string attached to the bob determines the pendulum's frequency. The longer the string, the lower the pendulum's frequency.

See for Yourself

Materials
string, 18 inches (45 cm)
washer with a hole, or any comparable weight
tape

What to Do
1. Tie one end of the string to the washer.
2. Tape the free end of the string to the edge of a table. Leave part of the end of the string free. This end of the string will be pulled to shorten the string.
3. Pull the washer to one side and release it. The washer should freely swing without touching anything (Figure 1).

Pendulum

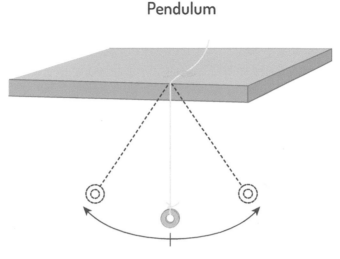

FIG 1

4. As the washer swings, slowly pull the end of the string to shorten it. As you shorten the string, observe the change in the frequency of the pendulum.

What Happened?

As the length of the string is shortened, the distance the bob swings gets shorter. Thus, it takes less time for the bob to swing back and forth. This means that, given the same interval of time, a shorter pendulum will swing back and forth more times than a longer pendulum. So, there is a relationship. The frequency of a shorter pendulum is higher than the frequency of a longer pendulum.

3. Coupled Pendulums

Coupled pendulums can be formed by two pendulums suspended from a common support. In this setup, energy from one swinging pendulum can be transferred through the medium connecting the two pendulums. As a result, one swinging pendulum will transfer energy to the second pendulum, starting it swinging. As the energy is transferred back and forth, one pendulum stops and the other swings, reversing the energy transfer. Through careful observation, a prediction can be made when one pendulum will stop and the other one will start. It looks a bit magical but it's not. It's all about the transfer of mechanical energy.

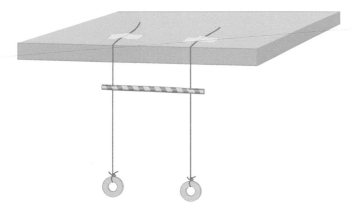

FIG 1

See for Yourself

Materials

string, 2 × 8 inch (20 cm) pieces

tape

ruler

scissors

straw

2 washers with holes, or any comparable weight

What to Do

1. Tie one end of each string to a washer.
2. Tape the free end of each string to the edge of a table. The strings need to be about 6 inches (15 cm) apart. The string lengths for both pendulums need to be the same.
3. Cut 6 inches (15 cm) from the straw, and then cut short slits in both ends of the straw.
4. At about 2 inches (5 cm) from the tops of the string, attach the straw. The string should slide into the slits on the ends of each straw. Make sure that the straw is parallel with the table edge and the lengths of the pendulums below the straw are equal.
5. Pull one of the pendulums toward you a short distance and release; it should swing under the table. Observe movement in both pendulums.

What Happened?

Pendulums of the same length have the same natural frequency, which is the number cycles or the back and forth movements the pendulums would make in 1 second.

When only one pendulum is pulled and released, the end of the attached straw also moves back and forth with the same frequency. With each swing, the straw is giving the second pendulum small tugs. With each tug, the second pendulum moves a little higher. This happens at the expense of energy being transferred from the first pendulum. Thus, one pendulum slows down as the other pendulum swings higher. At this point there is a reverse of energy transfer. One might wonder why this back and forth transfer doesn't continue forever. The swinging pendulums are at the same time losing energy to other forms of energy, including heat and sound (air vibrations). Eventually, both pendulums will come to a standstill.

4. Sound Waves in Air

Sound waves travel through air in the form of waves called **longitudinal waves**. Sound waves transport energy as they travel through a medium. Sound waves are produced when an object, such as a plucked guitar string, vibrates. On one side of the string, the air molecules are compressed, or squeezed together, creating a high-pressure area. Areas of high pressure are called **compression**. At the same time on the opposite side of the string, a low-pressure area is produced allowing the air molecules to spread out, which is called **rarefaction**. Figure 1 models the compression and rarefaction of air surrounding a vibrating string that is represented by the red line. It is important to note that the air molecules around the string are moving back and forth but they never move far. Instead, each time the air molecules are compressed, they hit against other air molecules pushing them farther away from the string. The sound wave continues to move away from the source of the sound, the vibrating string, in all directions. Sound waves continue to move and bounce off surfaces until there is no more energy.

Sound Wave

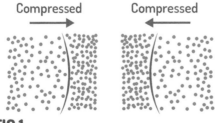

FIG 1

The compression and rarefaction of longitudinal waves can be demonstrated with a Slinky.

See for Yourself

Materials

Slinky

What to Do

1. Lay the Slinky on a table.
2. Hold the ends of the Slinky with your hands and stretch the Slinky so that it is about 2 feet (60 cm) long.
3. Holding one end of the Slinky stationary, push the opposite end inward about 4 inches (10 cm) and then pull outward again (Figure 2). Observe the movement of the coils in the Slinky.

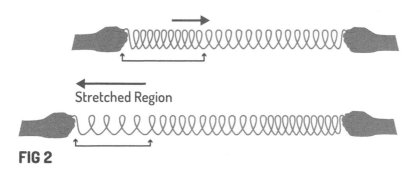

Stretched Region

FIG 2

What Happened?

Compressing the coils models the compression of air molecules when a vibrating object pushes on air molecules. As the object is pushing air together on one side, at the same time, on the opposite side, the air molecules are spreading apart. Stretching the coils models the rarefaction of air.

The compression of the coils sends a visible wave down the Slinky, modeling the way the air molecules behave when bumping into the next air molecules, and the next, and so on. At the end of the Slinky, the waves are bounced back. This back and forth movement continues but it will slow down over time until stopping, due to a loss of energy. The coils compress and stretch apart as the wave passes through the coils. At the secured end, the wave bounces back, sending the wave in the opposite direction. The person holding the end of the Slinky can feel the energy of the modeled sound wave because the last coil pushes against their hand. This back and forth movement occurs several times. Likewise, sound waves also bounce off of objects. Sound waves are absorbed by soft surfaces and reflected by hard surfaces. Figure 3 compares compression and rarefaction in the Slinky to a sound wave in air.

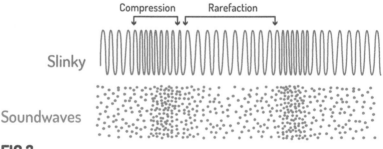

FIG 3

5. Pressure Waves

Sound waves are also called **pressure waves** because they increase and decrease in pressure as they move through a medium. An area where the pressure is greatest and the medium is squeezed together is called **compression**. An area of decreased pressure, where the medium is stretched out, is called **rarefaction**. Sound waves are initiated when a force (a push or pulling motion) is applied to a medium that can **vibrate**, meaning to move back and forth. Vibrating objects give surrounding air molecules a push, which starts a pressure wave that moves out in all directions like the ripples in a pond.

Blowing across the open mouth of an empty bottle starts a pressure wave in the bottle causing the air inside to vibrate. The air in the bottle will vibrate at a specific frequency, called its **natural frequency**, and the sound produced will be specific to that frequency. The height of the air column in an empty bottle is measured from the top of the bottle to its bottom. Adding water to the bottle will shorten the height of this air column. The sound waves bounce off the surface of the water in much the same way as they bounce off the bottom of the bottle. Thus, the sound heard depends on the height of the air column. As the height of the column decreases, the frequency of the sound produced increases. The highness or lowness of the sound, called the **pitch**, is directly related to the frequency of the sound.

FIG 1

See for Yourself

Materials

6 empty water bottles, same size and shape
water

What to Do

1. Support each empty bottle with your hand, and then blow across the top of each one.
2. Compare the sounds made by each bottle.
3. Change the height of the air column inside each bottle by adding varying amounts of water and compare the sounds that are produced.

18

What Happened?

The results of this experiment confirmed that as the height of a vibrating air column, which is closed at one end, decreases, the frequency of the sound produced increases. It also confirmed that the pitch of sound is directly related to the frequency of the sound. The lower the frequency, the lower the pitch, and vice versa. The empty bottle produces the lowest pitched sound because it has the air column with the greatest height; thus, the sound produced has the lowest frequency. By increasing the quantity of water added to the bottles, the height of the air column in each bottle was shortened, increasing the frequency of the sound waves, and so higher pitched sounds were produced.

6. Pitch

Pitch is a property of sound. Pitch describes the highness or lowness of a sound. The frequency of sound waves determines the pitch heard. Remember, sound is how pressure waves entering your ears are perceived by your brain. Not everyone perceives a specific sound the same. But all can agree that the lower the frequency, the lower the pitch, and the higher the frequency, the higher the pitch. Pitch has nothing to do with the loudness or softness of a sound.

A flute made from a drinking straw is a simple homemade instrument that, like all wind instruments, vibrates at a specific frequency. The source of the pressure wave that starts the air vibrating is the reed at one open end. The **reed** is made to vibrate by blowing on it. A straw flute is made with a double reed, consisting of two parts that vibrate, which sends a pressure wave into the straw causing an air column in the open tube to vibrate. The longer the straw, the longer the air column inside and the lower the frequency. This means a longer straw will produce a lower pitch. Conversely, decrease the length of the straw and there is an increase in both the frequency and pitch.

See for Yourself

Materials
bendy drinking straw
scissors
ruler

marking pen
helper

What to Do

1. With your fingers, flatten the short end above the accordion folds in the straw.
2. Figure 1 has marks indicating where to cut the straw to form the reed part of the straw flute. Once the two cuts have been made, cut the sharp point off to blunt the end.

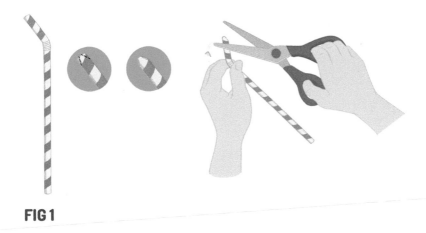

FIG 1

3. Moisten your lips, then place the reed in your mouth past your teeth and blow. If the flute is not producing sound, try drawing in the lips around the teeth rather than puckering them. Slightly lifting or lowering the straw flute can also help. Don't be too quick to give up. It might take a few tries to reach the goal of making a sound.

FIG 2

4. Once you have mastered playing the straw flute, ask your helper to cut small sections off the end of the straw as you continue testing the straw flute.

What Happened?

The length of the straw component of the flute affects the sound frequency. A shorter straw will have a higher frequency. The higher the frequency, the higher the pitch of the sound produced. Thus, as the straw was shortened, it produced a sound with a higher pitch.

7. Sound Transmission

Sound transmission is the movement of sound energy via longitudinal waves. In most cases, sound travels slowest in gases, faster in liquids and fastest in solids. Sounds are loudest near the source. Sound waves are produced by a vibrating object. Figure 1 shows how sound waves move out from a sound source through air. Notice that closest to the sound source, the compressed areas are very dark, but fade in color with distance from the speaker. The diagram shows that the spacing between the dark areas doesn't change. The equal spacing in the diagram illustrates that the frequency of sound doesn't change with distance, only the **amplitude** or energy of the wave decreases. Thus, the sound would be the loudest at position A, and softest at position C. This relationship is true with all sound waves. Also, the energy of the sound would travel farther through a solid than in air.

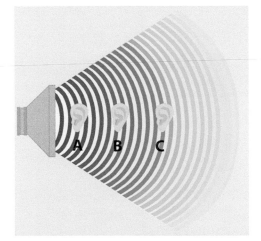

FIG 1

See for Yourself

Materials

2 metal spoons
string, 3 yards (1.8 m)
helper

What to Do

1. Tie the string around the handle of one of the spoons so the two ends of the string are about the same length.
2. Wrap the ends of the string around your index fingers. Let the string and spoon hang in a V shape.
3. Extend your arms in front of you as shown in Figure 2 so the spoon hangs freely without touching anything.

FIG 2

24

4. Ask your helper to use the second spoon to gently tap the hanging spoon (Figure 3). Make note of the sound produced by the spoon.

FIG 3

5. Stick your index fingers in your ears and lean forward so the hanging spoon dangles freely. Check to make sure the string is not touching any object.
6. Again, ask your helper to tap the spoon as before. Compare the two sounds.

What Happened?

Everything that vibrates sends out sound waves through the air in all directions. The frequency or pitch of the sound was the same each time the spoon was tapped. But, the amplitude, or loudness, of the sound was greater with your fingers and the string pressed into your ears. This is because when traveling through air, the sound waves move slower than when they travel through a solid. Thus, more sound waves reached your ears when they traveled up the string to your ears. Also, the string provided a direct route for the sound from the vibrating spoon to your ears.

8. The Effect of Mass on Sound

Mass is a measure of the amount of matter in an object. For example, some drinking glasses are thicker than others, thus they are more massive. In reference to sound, the more massive a vibrating object, the lower the frequency, and hence the pitch. The reverse is true if the mass decreases with a result of a higher frequency and higher pitch.

In this activity, water will be added to glasses to change their mass. Tapping on a glass with water will produce a sound with a certain frequency. It will be seen that increasing the mass of a glass and then tapping on it will produce a sound with a lower frequency. Altering the amount of water in the glass can produce different musical notes.

See for Yourself

Materials

6 drinking glasses of equal size and shape (the thinner the glass walls, the better)

water

food coloring

pencil

What to Do

1. Pour different amounts of water in five of the glasses. Leave one glass empty.
2. Using food coloring, make the water in each glass a different color.

27

Note: The coloring doesn't change the sound that will be produced. It merely helps to associate each glass with the sound it produces.

3. Gently tap each glass with the wooden end of a pencil.

4. Compare the sounds made by each glass with water to the sound produced by the empty glass. Determine which produces the highest and the lowest frequency.

FIG 1

An experimental challenge is to alter the amount of water in each glass to produce the notes to play a simple song.

What Happened?

The sound produced by tapping each glass was different depending on the amount of water it contained. The sound heard also depended on the sound produced by the glass; thus, an empty glass was used that vibrated the fastest when tapped, so it had the highest frequency and the note was high. A glass with water in it vibrated slower when tapped because the glass and water together had a greater mass. The greater the mass, the slower the vibrations of the glass when tapped. Slower vibrations mean a lower frequency of sound waves. The high and low musical notes produced are related to frequency. High notes are produced by high frequencies and low notes by low frequencies. Adjusting the level of water in a glass can result in notes that go up or down the musical scale.

9. Natural Frequency

Natural frequency is the frequency at which a material vibrates when hit, plucked, strummed, or somehow set into motion. When a tuning fork is struck, it vibrates at a specific frequency: its natural frequency. As a tuning fork vibrates, it causes the air around itself to vibrate, which produces the sound waves you hear. A simple motion, such as rubbing the rim of a glass, can cause it to vibrate at its natural frequency and produce sound.

See for Yourself

Materials

stemmed glass (this will work best if the glass is thin)
dish detergent
small bowl of water

What to Do

1. Remove excess oil from your hands and clean the rim of the glass by washing with dish detergent and rinsing well. Dry your hands and the stemmed glass thoroughly.
2. Place the glass on a table.
3. Hold the base of the glass against the table with your hand.
4. Wet the index finger of your free hand with water and move your wet finger in one direction around the rim of the glass pressing gently.

FIG 1

What Happened?

The glass starts to "sing." Washing your hands removes any oil that might act as a slippery lubricant. Rubbing a wet finger around the rim causes the glass to vibrate. Due to friction, your finger skips and pulls at the glass as it moves around the rim. Just in the way a tuning fork begins vibrating when struck, this irregular touching on the glass rim actually acts like tiny taps that cause the glass to begin vibrating. In turn, the air inside and outside the bowl of the glass is struck by these vibrations and begins to move back and forth in a wavelike pattern. These sound waves spread out in all directions from the vibrating glass. A musical tone can be heard. The pitch of the sound you hear is due to the natural frequency of the glass.

10. Neutral Atom

A **neutral atom** has no electric charge. **Atoms** are the building blocks of **matter**. Think of it as the stuff of which everything in the Universe is made. The center of an atom, called the **nucleus**, holds both **protons**, which are positively charged particles, and **neutrons**, which are particles with no charge. **Electrons** are negatively charged particles that spin around the nucleus at different distances called **energy levels**.

A neutral atom has an equal number of protons and electrons; thus, it has an overall net charge of zero. Much like the addition of +1 and −1 equals 0, the sum of one positive charge from one proton and one negative charge from one electron also equals zero.

The **Bohr model** of an atom looks much like a model of planets orbiting the Sun at different distances. Comparatively, in the Bohr model, negatively charged electrons orbit a positively charged nucleus in different energy levels. The Bohr model of an atom can be demonstrated with a paper model.

See for Yourself

Materials
blank paper
pencil
scissors
tape

What to Do

1. Fold the paper in half three times, once from top to bottom, and then from side to side, and last fold along a diagonal line so that the top folded edge meets the side fold as shown in Figure 1.

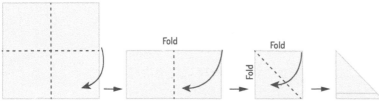

FIG 1

2. Draw five curved lines on the top layer of the folded paper.
3. Cut along each of the five curved lines. Keep the three indicated sections as shown in Figure 2.

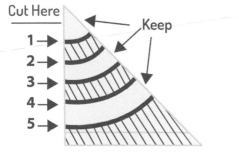

FIG 2

33

4. Unfold the three sections; write "6p+" and "6n" in the circle, which represents the six protons and six neutrons in the nucleus of the atom.

5. In the smaller ring, draw two electrons (e⁻) on opposite sides, and in the largest ring, draw four electrons (e⁻) randomly spaced and as far apart as possible.

6. Connect the three parts by taping the string to each as shown in Figure 3. Secure the end of the string to a surface so that the atom model can hang freely.

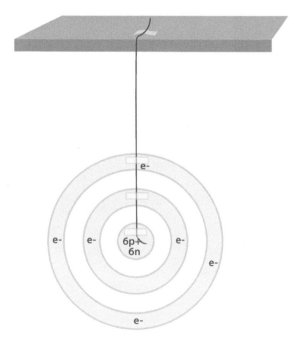

FIG 3

34

What Happened?

This Bohr model is of the element carbon (C). The carbon atom model is neutral because it has six positively charged protons (p^+) in its nucleus and six negatively charged electrons (e^-) in the rings, which represent energy levels. In the Bohr model, atoms may hold up to two electrons in the first ring and up to eight electrons in the second ring. Since there are only a total of six electrons in a neutral atom of carbon, two electrons are in the first energy level and the remaining four electrons spread out in the second energy level, which is the outer ring. The electrons in the outer energy level of an atom are called **valence electrons**. The atom model of carbon has an overall charge of zero; thus, it is a neutral atom.

11. Electric Current

An electric current is the movement of electrons. The faster the electrons move, the more kinetic energy they have. Kinetic energy of moving electrons can be called **electrical energy**. The strength of the current, or **flow rate**, is a measurement of the number of electrons moving past a point each second and is measured in **amperes (A)**. One ampere is equal to 6.24 quintillion (=6.24 million million million) electrons each second. You can model the flow rate of current electricity using grains of sand. Just as the flow rate of an electric current is measured in electrons per second, the flow rate of sand can be measured in the number of ounces of sand that flows per second.

See for Yourself

Materials
pencil
paper cup, 7 oz (210 mL)
masking tape
small grain sand
ruler
small bowl
timer
helper

What to Do
Note: This experiment works best on a dry day, because moist sand tends to stick together when the weather is humid.

1. Use the pencil to punch a hole in the center of the paper cup's bottom. The hole should equal the circumference of the pencil
2. Place a piece of tape over the hole in the cup.
3. Fill the cup to the top with sand. Rub the edge of the ruler across the top of the cup to make sure the surface of the sand is level.
4. Hold the cup 6 inches (15 cm) above the bowl.
5. Ask your helper to start the timer as soon as you remove the tape from over the hole in the cup. Stop the timer the instant the sand stops flowing from the cup.

FIG 1

6. Repeat the experiment four times, and then average the times taken from all the tests.

7. Calculate the flow rate of the sand using the follow-ing equation:

$$\text{Flow rate} = \frac{\text{volume of sand, oz} \left(\text{mL} \right)}{\text{average time, seconds}}$$

Note: The volume of the sand is equal to the volume of the cup used.

What Happened?

The flow of sand passing through the hole can be described as the volume measured in ounces (mL) of sand that passed a given point in one second. The flow rate of sand is not an exact model of the flow rate of electrons, but it does model measuring the flow rate of the material. The larger the hole in the cup, the greater will be the flow rate of sand. The same is true with an electric wire: the larger the diameter of the wire, the greater will be the current of electricity flowing through.

12. Conductors vs. Insulators

Conductors are materials through which an electric current can flow freely. **Insulators** do not allow an electric current to easily pass through. Conducting materials have a low **electro-negativity** rating, meaning **valence electrons** are loosely bound to atoms and free to move from one atom to the next. These wandering electrons are called **free electrons**. This movement or flow of electrons in a conductor is called an electric current. But free electrons don't move unless they are given a push, which can come from a **battery**. Batteries are storehouses for chemical energy, which is a type of potential energy. When a battery is connected to a conductor, the chemical energy in the battery is converted to electrical energy. A battery provides the "push" that results in the movement of free electrons in the conductor. Batteries have two ends called the **terminals**; the end that releases electrons is called the **negative terminal**, and the end that receives electrons is called the **positive terminal**. When connected to a conductor, free electrons move in one direction out of the negative terminal of the battery through the conductor and back to the positive terminal. This path is called an **electric circuit** (or simply a **circuit**). Examples of good conductors are metals, such as copper and aluminum, that have loosely bound outer electrons. Examples of good insulators are nonmetals, which have a high electronegativity, thus their valence electrons are more tightly bound to their atoms, resulting in their suitability as an insulative material. Rubber, paper, and plastics are examples of insulators.

See for Yourself

Materials

aluminum foil 24 × 12 inches (60 × 30 cm)

scissors

duct tape

D cell battery

flashlight bulb

wooden spring-type clothespin

testing materials: rubber band, paper, coin, metal paper-clip, metal washer

The battery can get hot at the point of connection with the aluminum strips. Remember to take your demonstration apart when finished.

What to Do

1. Fold the aluminum foil in half lengthwise five times to form a thin 24 inch (60 cm) strip. Cut the strip in half to form two 12 inch (30 cm) strips.
2. Tape one end of each of the aluminum strips snugly to opposite ends of the battery.
3. Wrap the free end of one of the metal strips around the metal base of the flashlight bulb. Hold the aluminum strip in place with the clothespin.
4. Before proceeding, check that the aluminum strips do not touch each other, otherwise the bulb will not glow. Then make sure the bulb will glow by touching the tip on the bulb's bottom to the free end of the other aluminum strip. If it doesn't glow, check all connections. If the bulb still doesn't glow, try replacing the bulb or battery with a new one.

40

5. Determine the conductivity of a coin using the following procedure:

- Lay the coin on top of the free end of the aluminum foil strip connected to the battery.
- Holding the clothespin, touch the metal tip on the bottom of the flashlight bulb to the top of the coin. The bulb will glow if the coin is made of conducting material.

6. Repeat step #5 using the other testing materials.

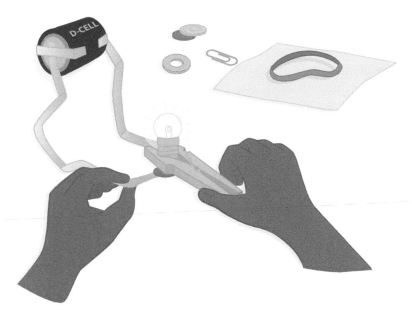

FIG 1

41

What Happened?

In this demonstration setup, there is a gap between the aluminum foil strip and the lightbulb. This gap constitutes a break in the circuit. It prevents the lightbulb from receiving a flow of electrons, hence the bulb remains unlit.

The testing materials act as a bridge that connects the free end of one aluminum strip and the metal tip on the bottom of the flashlight bulb. If the material is conductive, an electric current flows from the battery through the aluminum strip into and out of the blub, and back to the battery via the other aluminum strip. This is called a **closed circuit**, meaning there is a continuous cycle of electricity. Nonconductive testing materials may physically connect the aluminum strip to the bulb, but they block the flow of electric current from the battery. These materials can be classified as insulators. Insulators cause a break in the circuit. This is called an **open circuit**.

When testing the materials listed, the coin, paperclip, and metal washer were the only materials that completed the circuit, allowing the electrons to move and causing the bulb to glow. Thus, the metal materials were the only conductors. All of the metals on the testing list proved to be good conductors, but not all metals in the Earth are good conductors. The materials that do not allow the electrons to move are insulators. The rubber band and paper are classified as insulators because they do not complete the circuit.

13. LED

A light-emitting diode or **LED** is an electrical device that emits light when an electric current passes through it. In Greek, "*di*" means two. LEDs have two legs or leads, which are conductive wires through which electricity enters and leaves the LED. Generally, one LED lead is longer than the other, which is the positive lead. For an LED to glow, an electric current must flow from a negative battery terminal to the negative lead of the LED, through the LED, out the positive LED lead and back to the positive battery terminal. Remember, for current to flow through an LED, the longer, positive lead must be connected to the positive terminal of a battery.

Incandescent light bulbs produce light by heating a fine wire called a **filament** inside the bulb. In comparison, LEDs produce almost no heat, last much longer, and use less electrical energy. When the LED is connected to a battery, energy in the form of light particles called **photons** is emitted. Photons are packets of light energy. The color of the light emitted by an LED depends on the energy of the photons released by the LED.

See for Yourself

Materials

3 mm LED bulb, 3.0 V
lithium coin cell battery 3.0 V

Do not use any other type of battery for this investigation, as you could be burned. Coin cell batteries contain lead and are harmful if swallowed. Take care to store them out

43

of reach of young children. Make sure to insulate battery terminals with vinyl tape when disposing of or storing them to avoid any discharge.

What to Do

1. Investigate the LED and the coin battery:
   - Compare the leads on the LED.
   - Compare the two sides of the battery. Make note of the side marked with a plus (+) sign.
2. Holding the battery, slip the coin battery between the two LED leads. Press the leads against the battery with your fingers. Make note of what happens.
3. Repeat step 2 turning the battery over.
4. Repeat this investigation making note of how the LED leads must be connected to the battery for it to light up.

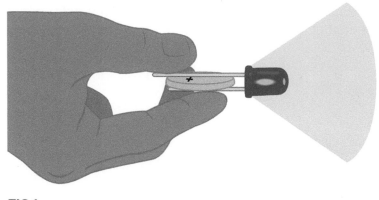

FIG 1

What Happened?

The LED's leads must be connected to the correct battery terminals for the LED to emit light. Commonly, the type of LED used in this investigation has one longer lead that is positive. This positive lead must make connection with the positive side of the battery. When the LED glows, you have confirmed that the LED will glow when the leads are correctly connected to a battery, and that the battery is a source of stored energy. While the positive LED lead must connect to a battery's positive terminal, it doesn't have to be a direct contact, meaning conductive wire may be attached to the LED so that the LED is part of a circuit.

14. Electrochemical Energy

Electrochemical energy is stored chemical energy, which is a type of potential energy that can be converted into electricity. **Dry cell batteries**, such as those used in cell phones and remote-control devices, all have stored chemical energy that produces current electricity (moving electrons). Electrochemical, "electro" refers to electrons, and chemicals are the source of the electrons. The type of battery, alkaline or acidic, is determined by the chemicals used. Although the chemical reactions can be a bit complex, for the purposes of this activity, it's important to know why the ends of a battery have different electric charges.

Figure 1 shows the basic components of a battery. Know that it is not safe to open a battery. The contents can damage your skin. Looking carefully at the diagram, note that the metals used for the two terminals, the connectors usually found at opposite ends of the battery, are never in direct contact. Also, notice that the chemicals producing the positive and negative charges for the two terminals are separated. To create an electric circuit, a conducting material that connects the **anode** (positive terminal) and **cathode** (negative terminal) must be used for the two separate chemical reactions to occur. In this activity, an aluminum foil strip is the conducting material used to connect the two battery terminals, thus allowing an electric current to flow from one terminal to the other. When connected properly, electrons from the anode, or negative battery terminal, and free electrons in the metal strip are

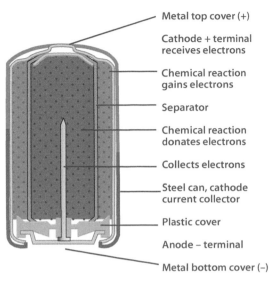

Metal top cover (+)

Cathode + terminal
receives electrons

Chemical reaction
gains electrons

Separator

Chemical reaction
donates electrons

Collects electrons

Steel can, cathode
current collector

Plastic cover

Anode – terminal

Metal bottom cover (–)

FIG 1

attracted to the cathode, or positive battery terminal. While it might seem that one reaction triggers the other, in reality, the reactions occur simultaneously because one cannot occur without the other.

If an incandescent light bulb is part of this circuit, the electrons pass through the bulb and then continue on to the cathode. An incandescent bulb has a very fine wire called a filament. This wire resists the movement of the electrons. This resistance causes the filament to get so hot that it glows, thus changing heat energy into light energy. In this example, electrical energy is converted into heat, much like quickly rubbing the palms of your hands together changes mechanical energy into heat energy.

See for Yourself

Materials

aluminum foil strip, 2 inches (5 cm) by 12 inches (30 cm)

flashlight bulb, incandescent

battery, 1.5 V D cell

What to Do

1. Fold the strip of aluminum foil in half lengthwise three times to form a thin strip ¼ inch (0.63 cm) wide.
2. Use the aluminum foil strip to connect the battery and bulb so that the bulb glows.

Note: Current flows into the bulb in one place and out at another (Figure 2). It doesn't matter at which point the electrons enter and exit the bulb. One point is the metal tip on the bottom and the other is the metal around the base of the bulb.

Always disassemble your circuit when you have finished.

What Happened?

When the electric current flows in a complete circuit from one battery terminal, through the bulb, and back into the opposite terminal, the bulb glows. One way to accomplish this is to stand the anode (–) end of the battery on one end of the aluminum strip and then wrap the opposite end of the aluminum strip around the metal neck of the bulb. To complete the circuit, stand the metal tip on the bottom of the bulb on top of the cathode (+) end of the battery (Figure 3). When an electric circuit is complete, parts can get hot.

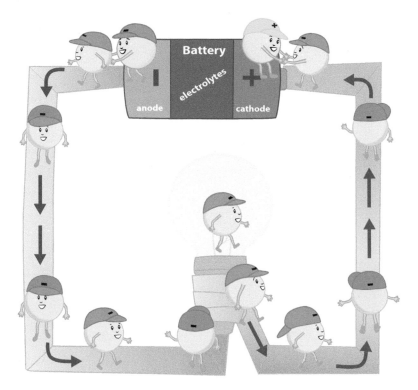

FIG 2

The incandescent light bulb uses heat to produce light (Figure 3). This heat is produced when the thin tungsten wire resists the motion of electrons, thus electrons smash into tungsten atoms causing them to vibrate. **Temperature** is a measure of the average kinetic energy of these vibrating particles. An increase in temperature results in an

FIG 3

increase in **thermal energy** (heat energy). Some of this heat energy energizes free electrons and they move farther from the nucleus to a higher energy level. These electrons quickly release this extra energy in the form of light photons and return to their **ground state**, normal position.

15. Polarizing an Insulator

In reference to atomic particles, such as atoms or molecules, polarizing means to separate their positive and negative charges. Insulators are materials that do not have free electrons that can move from one atom to the next. For this reason, insulators do not conduct electricity. To polarize, or separate, positive and negative charges in an insulator, one only needs to bring some object with a charge nearby, but not touching, the surface of the insulator, such as the wall in Figure 1. Note that, in Figure 1 the neutral, or uncharged

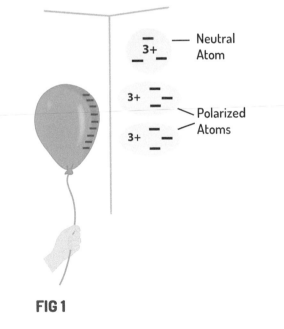

Neutral Atom

Polarized Atoms

FIG 1

atoms, in the wall have three protons in the center with three electrons distributed around them. Note that the neutral atom has a more spherical shape. When the negatively charged balloon is brought near the wall, there is an **electrostatic repulsion** between the like charges, negative and negative. This repulsive force is great enough to cause the electrons to move back from the wall's surface. This leaves the surface that faces the charged balloon with a positive charge. Note that the electrons in the polarized atom are not leaving the atom, instead they are just more concentrated in one area.

In Figure 2, the negatively charged balloon clings to the positively charged surface of the wall. The force of attraction

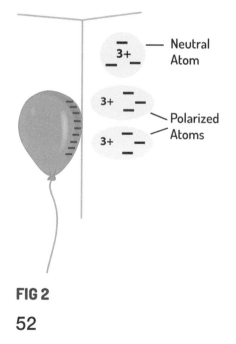

FIG 2

between unlike charges, positive and negative, is called the **electrostatic attraction**.

The buildup of charges in one place is called **static electricity**, which is a form of **potential electrical energy**.

The force of repulsion and the force of attraction between charges can be strong enough to cause movement of some lightweight objects, such as pieces of paper.

See for Yourself

Materials
modeling clay
pushpin
scissors
tissue paper (if not available, use another lightweight paper)
clear plastic cup (optional)
polystyrene plate
washcloth (a cotton t-shirt or wool scarf will substitute)

What to Do
1. Roll a dime-sized piece of clay into a ball and press it onto a table.
2. Push the plastic end of the pushpin into the clay, leaving the point sticking straight up.
3. Cut a piece from the tissue paper, about 1 inch (2.5 cm) square. Fold the paper in half.
4. Open the folded paper slightly and balance it on top of the pinpoint as shown in Figure 3.
5. Carefully position the plastic cup over the pin. The plastic cup prevents air motion from moving the paper.

6. Charge the polystyrene plate by rubbing it back and forth with the washcloth five to six times.

7. Hold the charged plate near, but not touching, the plastic cup.

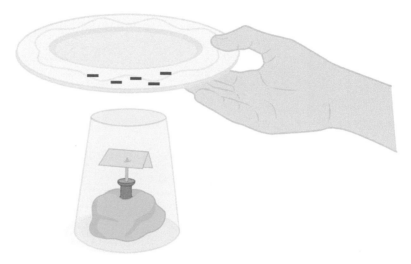

FIG 3

What Happened?

A polystyrene plate has a higher affinity for electrons than a washcloth. Rubbing the polystyrene plate with the wash-cloth is an example of **charging by contact**; the rubbing off of electrons. The electrons are rubbed off the washcloth and build up on the plate. Thus, the plate acquires a neg-ative static electric charge and the washcloth is left with a positive static electric charge. Paper is an insulator. When the negatively charged plate is held near the paper, it causes the atoms on the surface that are facing the charged plate to be polarized. Thus, there is a separation of the positive and negative charges within the atoms. Being an insulator, the electrons in the cloud of electrons swarming around the atoms near the surface of the charged plate move farther back from this surface. If the paper in this investigation is not too heavy, this electrostatic force of attraction can cause the paper to fall off the pin.

16. Polarizing a Conductor

Polarizing is a process of separating the positive and negative charges in atoms. Conductors have electrons that can move from one atom to the next; these are called free electrons. Metals are good conductors. Figure 1 represents the polarization of atoms in a metal by bringing a negatively charged balloon near but not touching the metal's surface. Unlike insulators, the electrons in metals can actually move from one atom to the next. Thus, the electrostatic repulsion between the negative charges on the balloon and the negative electrons in the atoms results in the free electrons moving away from the surface atoms. If the metal is an empty can, the outside surface near the negatively charged balloon

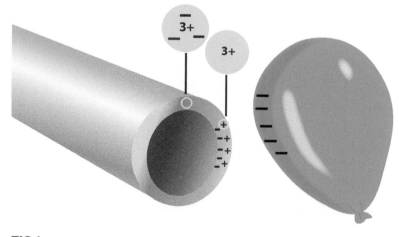

FIG 1

would be positive while the inside surface would be negative. While the metal has been polarized, its overall charge is zero because it still has the same number of positive charges as negative charges. They are just redistributed.

See for Yourself

Materials
balloon
wool scarf or cotton t-shirt
empty metal soda can

What to Do
1. Inflate the balloon and tie it.
2. Lay the can on its side on a smooth surface.
3. Rub the balloon with the scarf five or more times.
4. Hold the balloon near, but not touching, the can. Slowly move the balloon away from the can. Observe any movement in the can (Figure 2).
5. Repeat the experiment using the positively charged scarf.

What Happened?

The can rolls on its side toward both the negatively charged balloon as well as the positively charged scarf. As the negatively charged balloon nears the neutrally charged metal can, the electrons in the atoms of the can are **repelled** from the surface leaving the surface facing the balloon with a positive charge. Opposite charges attract each other; thus, the positive surface charge on the can is attracted to the negative charge on the balloon. This electrostatic force of attraction is enough to cause the can to roll. Repeating the experiment using the positively charged wool scarf

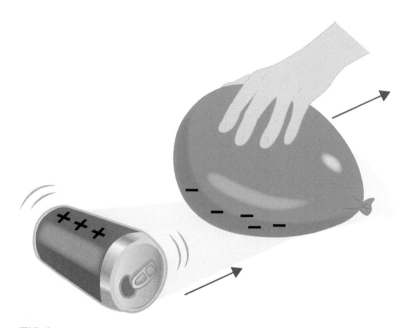

FIG 2

appears to produce the same results. The can rolls toward the scarf. It might be surprising to note that although the results appeared identical, the electrostatic charges on the materials were, in fact, different. The positively charged scarf attracts the electrons in the can's surface; thus, they move closer to the surface. The electrostatic attraction between the positive scarf and negative surface of the can results in the can rolling toward the scarf.

17. Electroscope

An electroscope is an instrument, invented in 1748, that is used to detect the presence of an electric charge on an object. A simple homemade electroscope can be made by attaching two thin metal strips to the ends of a bent piece of conducting wire. When a negatively charged object is held near the top of the wire, the two metal strips move apart due to the movement of electrons in the conducting wire and their collection on the metal strips giving the metal strips a negative charge. The same result occurs if the charged object has a positive charge.

See for Yourself

Materials
pushpin
2 strips of thin aluminum foil ½ inch × 2 inches (1 cm × 5 cm)
needle-nosed pliers
large metal paper clip
modeling clay
clean, dry, transparent, quart jar
circle of stiff paper to cover the top of the jar
balloon, 9 inch (23 cm)
wool scarf or cotton t-shirt
adult helper

What to Do

1. With adult assistance, use the pliers to reshape a metal paperclip as shown in Figure 1.

FIG 1

2. Use the pushpin to make two holes in the center of the paper disk.
3. Push the ends of the paper clip through the hole in the paper disk and then bend the ends upward to make hooks.
4. Use the pushpin to make a hole in one of the narrow ends of each strip of aluminum foil.
5. Hang the foil strips on the wire hooks, and then place the paper disk over the mouth of the jar with the metal strips hanging inside the jar. The strips are to hang freely not touching the jar.
6. Inflate the balloon and rub it back and forth on the wool scarf five to six times.
7. Hold the balloon very close but not touching the loop, and then move it slowly away from the loop.
8. Repeat step #7 using the charged scarf instead of the balloon.

FIG 2

What Happened?

When the charged balloon was held near the metal wire, the aluminum strips moved apart. When the charged balloon was moved away, the strips returned to their original position, hanging down. The same thing occurred when the charged scarf was used.

The negatively charged balloon did not transfer electrons to the metal wire. Instead, it induced a movement of the free electrons in the metal loop of the paperclip to the aluminum strips. Thus, the aluminum strips took on a surface negative static charge and repelled each other.

61

Without the charged balloon, the displaced electrons returned to their normal position and there was no longer a separation of charges. The metal strips will also separate when using the positively charged scarf, but for a different reason. This time the electrons were attracted toward the positively charged scarf, and this included the electrons in the metal strips. Thus, the metal loop had more of a negative charge and the metal strips had a positive surface charge. There is a repulsive electrostatic force between like charges. Remember, a charged object brought near, but not touching, a conductive material only induces a separation of charges or polarizes the material. But the overall net charge of the material remains zero because it still has the same number of positive and negative charges.

18. Triboelectric Effect

The triboelectric effect is a method of producing static electricity. This method requires the materials to be in contact with each other and then separated. Another requirement is for one material to have more affinity for electrons than the other. Thus, when separated, one material will pull electrons from the other, giving it a negative charge. The material that loses electrons has an overall positive charge. This is not polarization, where positive and negative charges are separated producing surface charges. Instead the separated materials have an overall charge because of having more electrons than protons, or, vice versa, more protons than electrons. Latex, like the material in a balloon, has a greater tendency to gain electrons while your skin has a greater tendency to lose electrons. This means that if you rub a latex balloon with your hand, static electricity will be produced on your skin as well as on the latex. Your skin will have a positive charge, while the latex would have a negative charge. Thus, the balloon and your hand would have an electrostatic attraction to each other.

See for Yourself

Materials
round balloon, 9 inches (22.5 cm)
string, 12 inches (30 cm)
tape

What to Do

1. Inflate the balloon and tie a knot in its end. Attach the 12 inch (30 cm) piece of string to the balloon, and then tape the free end of the string to the edge of a table.
2. Wash and dry your hands so they are clean and very dry.
3. Sit on the floor and slowly move your hand toward the balloon being careful not to make contact and make note of any movement of the balloon.
4. Hold the balloon in one hand and quickly rub your other hand back and forth across the surface of the balloon eight to ten times. Do not touch anything with this hand until you complete step #6.
5. Release the balloon and allow it to hang freely.
6. Hold the hand that was rubbed against the balloon near, but not touching, the balloon (Figure 1). Observe any movement of the balloon.

What Happened?

Before rubbing the hanging balloon, it did not move unless the movement of your hand sent a wave of air toward the balloon.

The atoms in your hand as well as in the balloon are neutral, meaning they have an equal number of negative electrons and positive protons. When your hand rubbed the balloon, electrons from your skin were attracted by the latex in the balloon. When you removed your hand from the balloon, your hand was left with a positive charge and the balloon was negatively charged. This was apparent because the balloon was attracted to your hand.

FIG 1

According to the law of charges, unlike charges attract. This attraction between unlike charges is called **electrostatic attraction**.

65

19. Adhesion: Charging by Contact

Adhesion is the attraction between two dissimilar particles or surfaces, such as tape stuck on a surface. While in contact, there can be an exchange of electrons from one surface to the other. When separated, one surface will have an excess of electrons, taking on a negative charge, while the other will have a deficit of electrons, leaving it with a positive charge. Adhesion is an example of the **triboelectric effect** for producing static electricity.

See for Yourself

Materials
index card, 4 × 6 inches (10 × 15 cm)
cellophane tape ¾ inch (1.9 cm) wide
helper

What to Do
1. Lay the index card on a table.
2. Pull off about 6 inches (15 cm) of tape and stick the tape across the index card, sticking the ends of the tape to the table as shown in Figure 1.
3. Repeat step #2 placing three additional pieces of tape across the card so they slightly overlap leaving no gaps between the tape pieces.

66

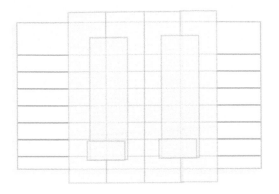

FIG 1

4. Pull off another piece of tape about 6 inches (15 cm) long. Stick this tape on top of the tape across the card. Fold the end of the tape back onto itself to form a lip to grasp the tape.

5. Repeat step #4, using a second piece of tape.

6. Rub both the top pieces of tape so that they are firmly pressed against the tape beneath them.

7. Grasping it securely by its folded end, quickly pull off one of the top tape pieces.

8. Ask a helper to pull off the other top piece of tape.

9. Hold the two pieces of tape near but not touching, and then hold the two tapes near but not touching the tape across the index card. Make note of the movement of the two tape pieces.

What Happened?

When the two TOP pieces of tape were pulled off the BOT-TOM pieces of tape, they became charged. Since both top pieces were treated the same, they both have the same charge. Like charges always repel; thus, when held near each other the two TOP pieces of tape will move away from each other (Figure 2). This electric force of repulsion is called an **electrostatic repulsion**.

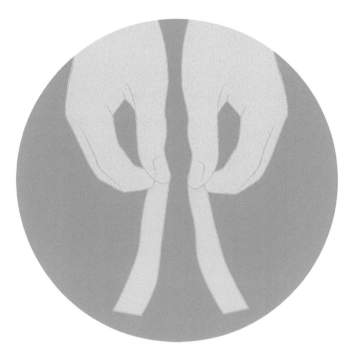

FIG 2

68

Separating the TOP and BOTTOM pieces of tape gave a positive charge to one and a negative charge to the other. Opposite charges always attract; thus, the TOP and BOTTOM tape pieces are attracted to each other by an electric force called an **electrostatic attraction**.

This activity demonstrates how static electricity can be produced by adhesion. While this activity did not identify the type of charge of the tape pieces, it can easily be determined which tape pieces had like charges, and which pieces had opposite charges.

Scientists have tested different materials and have concluded that the sticky bottom of cellophane tape has more of a tendency to lose electrons than does the smooth top surface. Thus, when separated, the sticky TOP piece of tape has a positive charge and the smooth BOTTOM has a negative charge.

20. Light Energy

Light energy is a form of **radiation**, which is wave energy that can travel through space. To be specific, light energy is electromagnetic radiation. There are seven types of light radiation and each has a specific range of frequency and **wavelength** (the distance between one wave and the next). These types of radiation, which are listed from the greatest energy having the highest frequency and shortest wavelength to the least energy with the lowest frequency and longest wavelength, are gamma rays, X-rays, ultraviolet light, visible light, infrared light, microwaves, and radiowaves. No matter what type of radiation, light energy is transferred by waves, but unlike water waves and sound waves, light waves need no medium to move through. Light can travel through space. Light energy travels at a speed of 670,000,000 m/hr (300,000,000 m/s) and always travels in a straight line.

See for Yourself

Materials
4 index cards, 4 × 6 inches (10 × 15 cm)
flashlight
scissors
modeling clay
ruler

What to Do

1. Cut 1-inch (2.5-cm) square notches from the center of one edge of each of the three index cards. Make sure to leave one of the four index cards uncut. The uncut index card will be used as a screen.

2. Use the clay as a stand to position the index cards upright about 4 inches (10 cm) apart with the notches aligned in a straight line.

3. Lay the flashlight in front of the card so that its beam of light will pass through the notch in the card facing it.

4. Use clay to position the index card screen at the end opposite the flashlight.

5. Darken the room and turn the flashlight on. Observe any light pattern on the paper screen.

6. Move the index cards so that the notches are not in a straight line.

7. Observe any light pattern on the paper screen.

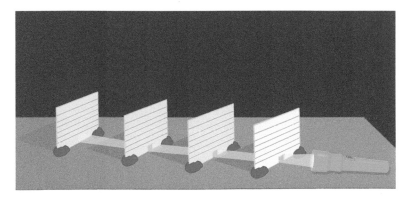

FIG 1

FIG 2

What Happened?

A beam of light from the flashlight travels in a straight line through the notches in the cards when the notches are in line with each other. After passing through the third notch, the beam of light continues until it hits the white paper index card screen. A bright circle of light appears on the screen, with some scattered light around it. When the notched cards were not in alignment, the beam of light passed through the notch on the first index card but was blocked from reaching and illuminating the screen by the other cards in its path. Instead, some of the light rays in the light beam were absorbed by the cards and some were reflected off the cards. As observed, light rays travel in a straight line until they hit an object.

72

21. Light Transmission

Light transmission is the moving of light energy and its interaction with different mediums. This transmission can be redirected, slowed, reduced, and even stopped when light is reflected, refracted, or absorbed by a material's molecules. **Reflect** means to bounce off of a surface. **Refract** means to change direction when entering a medium. **Absorption** means to take in and hold the energy. Unless otherwise indicated, **incident light** will refer to visible light that strikes a surface.

Transparent materials allow light to pass through with no absorption and no change in energy of the light. While light may cause the atoms or molecules in a transparent material to vibrate, the path of the light and its energy does not change. On occasion, there can be some reflection of visible light from the surface of transparent materials. This is why you can see your reflection in a glass window.

Opaque materials do not allow light to pass through. When visible light rays strike an opaque material, the surface molecules absorb and reflect the light. The light rays do not travel through the opaque material.

Translucent materials allow visible light to pass through, but the light is refracted internally. Refraction means that the light rays enter the material at one angle and exit at a new angle, or simply, they change direction. This causes an object that is viewed through the translucent material to be blurred and even distorted.

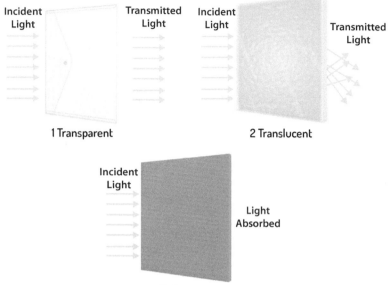

Incident Light — Transmitted Light

1 Transparent

Incident Light — Transmitted Light

2 Translucent

Incident Light — Light Absorbed

3 Opaque

FIG 1

See for Yourself

Materials
cardboard
wax paper
plastic folder, colorless see-through
helper

What to Do

1. One by one, hold the plastic folder, wax paper, and cardboard pieces in front of one of your eyes.
2. Look through the materials and note any differences in how objects in the room appear.
3. Ask your helper to repeat step #1 as you observe their face from behind each material (Figure 2).

1 Transparent

2 Translucent

3 Opaque

FIG 2

75

What Happened?

There is little or no change in appearance when things are observed through a transparent material such as plastic. Translucent materials, such as the wax paper, make objects look dull and blurred. Nothing can be seen through the cardboard, which is opaque.

In order for a person to see an object, the surface of the object must reflect light back to the eyes. The clear plastic folder is an example of a transparent material. Transparent means that light moves straight through the material. This light bounces off the reflected surface of the object and passes directly back through the transparent material to your eyes. Translucent materials, such as the wax paper, are not the same throughout, thus different parts of the wax paper refract the light at different angles. When these light waves reflect off objects, they return back through the paper and the light rays are refracted a second time. Some shower doors and bathroom windows are examples of translucent materials. Stained glass windows are also translucent. When viewed through translucent materials, objects look blurred or fuzzy. Cardboard is an opaque material that doesn't allow light to pass through. Instead, opaque materials absorb and reflect visible light. Since no light passes through and none is reflected back to your eyes, nothing on the opposite side of opaque materials can be seen.

22. Light Waves

Light waves are **transverse waves**, which are shaped like water waves. But, unlike water waves, light waves are not mechanical waves. **Mechanical waves** are formed in a medium, such as water waves in water and sound waves in air. The medium vibrates as the wave energy moves through it. Light waves need no medium through which to travel, such as waves of radiant energy, which travel from the Sun through space to Earth. It takes an average of 8 minutes and 20 seconds for radiation (light energy) leaving the Sun to reach Earth. At a speed of 299,792,458 m/s (about 300,000 km/s), light can travel around the Earth seven and a half times in one second. Light waves have the shape of transverse waves and can be easily modeled.

See for Yourself

Materials

Slinky, about 4 inches (10 cm)
helper

What to Do

1. On the floor, have your helper hold one end of the Slinky while you hold the other end. Stretch the Slinky to about four times its length.

2. While your helper holds one end of the Slinky securely in a stationary position, move the free end left and right several times. As you move the Slinky back and forth, observe the resulting movement in the coils of the Slinky.

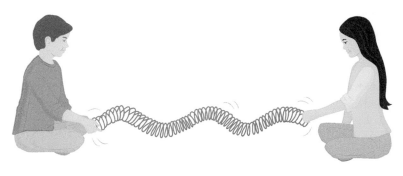

FIG 1

3. Using Figure 2, identify the different parts of the wave you produce with the Slinky.

Transverse Wave

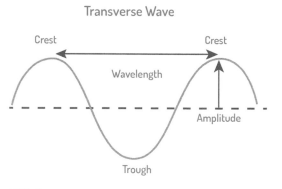

FIG 2

What Happened?

Shaking the Slinky left to right (back and forth) produces transverse waves that look like water waves. You start the

78

wave motion by moving one end back and forth. This energy moves to the opposite end of the Slinky, creating waves as it travels. At the stationary end, the wave energy bounces off your helper's hand and reverses its direction. If the forward and reflected waves are **in phase**, meaning that the crests and troughs match up, the amplitude of the wave where the two meet will be higher. The Slinky is moving, but it is not advancing forward. Instead, the energy is being transferred from one end to the other. By using your energy to start the Slinky moving, you were essentially doing work. Moving materials have kinetic energy. The kinetic energy of the Slinky is being transferred through it, which results in transverse waves forming and reforming as the energy travels from one end of the Slinky to the other.

23. Interference in Thin Films

Interference in physics means two waves superpose to form a resultant wave. **Superpose** means to overlap. The two types of interference, constructive and destructive, are shown in Figure 1. **Constructive interference** occurs when waves are in phase, meaning they are aligned with their crests and troughs overlapping. The resultant wave from constructive interference has a greater amplitude. **Destructive interference** is when two waves are **out of phase**, meaning they are opposite, or not aligned. These waves can cancel each other out, thus no wave is produced or a resultant wave is produced with a lesser amplitude. White light has all the colors of the visible light **spectrum**, but the diagram represents only one color, blue. The waves of blue light strike the surface of a very, very thin film of oil floating on water. Part of the blue light reflects off of the oil's surface and the rest of the blue light refracts, because it slows down, as it enters the denser oil. This light moves through the oil until it hits the oil–water boundary. Again, the light divides with part of it reflecting back to the top layer where the light, reentering the air, joins the other light that reflects from the oil's surface.

These two waves strike photoreceptors in the eye that send messages to the brain. It is the brain that actually superposes the wave messages, thus interpreting the combination of the two waves. The thickness of the oil film determines whether the second reflected wave is in phase or out of phase with the first reflected wave. The thicker the film the more time the light is traveling in the oil, which

Thin Film Light Interference

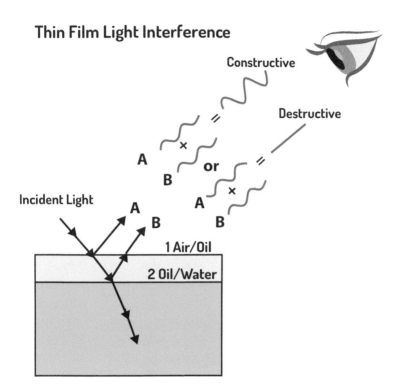

FIG 1

affects whether the waves are in phase or out of phase. When white light strikes a thin film, the surface will exhibit an array of colors.

See for Yourself

Materials

bowl
water

clear nail polish

desk lamp or flashlight

What to Do

1. Fill the bowl about half full with water.
2. Place the bowl of water on a table away from direct lighting.
3. Hold the brush from the polish bottle over the bowl of water and allow one drop of liquid polish to fall into the water.
4. Hold the light source on the opposite side of the bowl from you. The light needs to strike the surface of the water at an angle as shown in Figure 2. Change the angle of the light until you see colors in the thin film of nail polish on the surface of the water.

What Happened?

The nail polish spreads out forming a very thin film on the water's surface. When light strikes the surface of this film at an angle, a rainbow of colors is seen in the thin film. Part of the light striking the surface of the film is reflected. This reflected light is superposed, or joined, by the light that enters the film and is reflected off its bottom layer. The colors that are seen depend on how the light waves interfere with each other. Constructive interference occurs when the waves superpose to form a wave with greater amplitude. Destructive interference occurs when the waves superpose forming a wave with reduced amplitude. Total destructive interference subtracts the color. The colors of the thin film's surface are dependent on the thickness of the film. A thick film cancels out longer wavelengths in the red range. As the film gets thinner, first yellow, then green, and last blue wavelengths are canceled. The resulting colors are a combination of the colors that were not canceled by destructive interference.

FIG 2

Also, there are degrees of constructive interference that produce bright to dim colors. This can often be observed on a
pavement after rain. A thin sheet of oil from cars will float on
the water and appear to contain swirling colors. Now you
know the science behind this phenomenon.

24. Concave Lens

A lens is a curved transparent object, such as glass or plastic. A **concave lens** is thicker at its edges than at its center. **Ray diagrams** are drawings that represent the path of light rays. Ray diagrams for lenses illustrate the way that light rays travel through a lens. A line perpendicular and through the center of a lens is called the **principal axis**. Concave lenses are diverging lenses, meaning the parallel light rays entering the lens **diverge**, or bend away from the principal axis. When looking at an object through a concave lens, diverging rays appear to come from a point on the principal axis called the **focal point, F**. For concave lenses, the focal point is on the same side of the lens as the object, the source of light. Remember that light travels in a straight line; thus, all lines on a ray diagram are straight. The objective of ray diagrams is to locate the image formed by a lens.

See for Yourself

Materials
paper
pencil
ruler

What to Do
1. Draw a ray diagram for a concave lens using the following instructions:
   a. Draw a 6-inch (15-cm) line across the center of the paper. Label this line, "principal axis."

84

b. On the principal axis, starting at the zero point, mark each inch and label them in this order, from left to right: 2F', F', C, F, 2F.

c. On the principal axis, to the left of 2F', draw a 1-inch (2.5-cm) vertical arrow pointing up. This arrow represents an object, O. This is a distant object that is reflecting light toward the lens.

d. At the third inch mark, draw a 4-inch (10-cm) vertical line centered on the principal axis. This line represents the center of the double concave lens. Draw the lens around this center line with its narrow center being about ¼ inch (0.63 cm) wide where it crosses the principal axis line.

2. Draw a second line from the top of the object through the center of the lens.

3. Draw a line parallel to the principal axis from the top of the object (the arrow) to the center of the lens. At this point, the line diverges away from the principal axis. If this diverging line is extrapolated backward, it should pass through F', the focal point on the object's side of the lens. Use a dashed line to draw this extrapolated line.

4. Draw a vertical arrow pointing up from the principal axis to the point where the two lines meet on the same side as the object. This arrow represents the image of the object.

What Happened?

In Figure 1, two light rays from a distant object (O) are shown passing through a concave lens. The parallel light rays diverge after passing through a concave lens. Rays passing through the center of the lens do not refract, but instead continue in a straight line. These two rays do not meet after exiting the concave lens; thus they do not form a **real image** that can be projected on a screen. If looking through a concave lens, light rays from the lens enter your eye and the lens of your eye refracts the rays onto the retina. A message from the retina is sent to your brain. The brain interprets the message and you see what is called a **virtual image**. A virtual image is not real and cannot be projected on a screen. Because the brain interprets the light rays as coming from a source and, since light travels in straight lines, the brain "follows" the light rays back to the point where it thinks they meet. You therefore see an image that is upright but diminished in size.

Concave Lens Ray Diagram

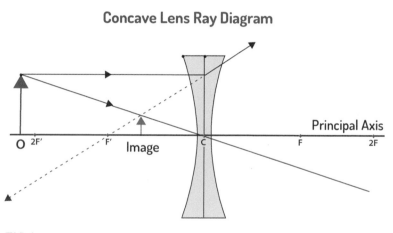

FIG 1

25. Convex Lens

A **lens** is a transparent material, such as glass or plastic, with curved surfaces. In a **convex lens**, the surface bulges outward in the center. A double convex lens bulges outward on both sides of the lens with the edges being thinner. Parallel light rays passing through a double convex lens are refracted. In any type of convex lens, parallel light rays that enter **converge**, or come together. These rays meet at a point beyond the lens called the **focal point**. Light rays passing through the center of a convex lens are not refracted, instead, they pass straight through. As with any lens, a line through the center of the lens is called the **principal axis**.

Distant light rays that pass through a convex lens converge to form a real, inverted, and diminished image on the far side of the lens from the light source. To construct a ray diagram for convex lenses, there are specific directions, which indicate the location of the image formed by the light rays.

See for Yourself

Materials
paper
pencil
ruler

What to Do

1. Draw a ray diagram for a convex lens using the following instructions:
   a. Draw a 6-inch (15-cm) line across the center of the paper. Label this line, "principal axis."
   b. Starting at the zero end, mark each inch and label them in this order, from left to right: 2F', F', C, F, 2F.
   c. On the principal axis to the left of 2F', draw a 1-inch (2.5-cm) vertical arrow pointing up. This arrow represents the object that is reflecting light toward the lens.
   d. At the third inch mark, draw a 4-inch (10-cm) line centered on the principal axis. This is the center of the double convex lens. Draw the lens around this centerline with the widest part ½ inch (1.27 cm) where it crosses the principal axis line.
2. Draw a line parallel to the principal axis from the top of the object (the arrow) to the center of the lens and then continue the line through and past the focal point (F) for about 2 inches (5 cm).
3. Draw a second line from the top of the object through the center of the lens. Extend the line until it crosses the line drawn in step #2.
4. Draw a third line from the top of the object through the focal point (F') on the object's side of the lens to the center of the lens. At this point, the line is parallel to the principal axis and should cross the point where the first two lines meet.
5. Draw a vertical arrow pointing down from the principal axis to the point where the three lines converge. This arrow represents the image as seen through the lens.

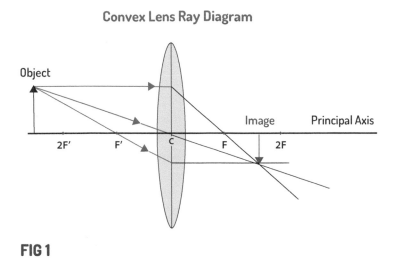

Convex Lens Ray Diagram

Object

Image   Principal Axis

2F′   F′   C   F   2F

FIG 1

What Happened?

Light rays from distant objects converge after passing through a convex lens forming a real image (can be projected on a screen) that is inverted and smaller than the object. Three rules for drawing ray diagrams for a convex lens can be stated:

1. Light rays parallel to the principal axis of a convex lens are refracted by the lens so that they pass through the focal point of the lens.

2. Light rays passing through the exact center of the lens are not refracted, but instead pass straight through.

3. Light rays passing through the focal point on the way to the lens are refracted by the lens so they exit parallel to the principal axis.

89

26. Plano-Convex Lens

A **plano-convex lens** is flat on one side and curved outward on the other side. When looking through the curved side of this lens at an object, what you see depends on how close the object is to the flat side of the lens. If the object being viewed is close to the flat surface, the object will appear larger. This is because light from the object changes direction when it passes through the lens. This is referred to as light refraction. Light entering the flat surface of the plano-convex lens is unaffected and does not refract until it passes through the curved surface. Here the light is refracted at an angle so that it passes through the focal point of the lens. Since all parallel rays passing through this lens converge, or come together, at the lens' focal point, it is called a converging lens. A water droplet on a flat surface forms a plano-convex lens.

See for Yourself

Materials
glossy page containing print from a magazine
eye dropper
water
round toothpick

What to Do
1. Lay the magazine page on a flat surface, such as a table.
2. Fill the eye dropper with water.
3. Add small drops of water to an area of the printed paper.
4. Look through the water drops at the letters they are covering. Compare the size of the letters viewed through

the water drop with the letters not covered by the water (Figure 1).

FIG 1

5. Use the toothpick to move 2 or more individual drops of water together, and then repeat step #4.

What Happened?

The drop of water is curved on the top and flat on its bottom side that is resting on the paper. The outer surface curves outward. The water droplet acts like a plano-convex lens, which is flat on one side and curved outward on the opposite side. The water drop lens magnifies the type underneath it. This virtual image is merely interpreted by your brain from messages sent from your eyes. Although others might see the same thing, the image is not real. Real images can be projected onto a screen.

The ray diagram in Figure 2 shows how the light rays form a virtual image. Notice the lines coming together to form the image are dashed instead of solid. This means they are not real. Instead, when looking through the water droplet, the light rays exiting the lens and entering your eyes do not come together, thus they do not form a real image on the retina of your eye. Since the human brain interprets that light rays come from a source and that light travels in a straight line, it "follows" the light rays back to a point where they meet. Thus, the virtual image is an optical illusion.

The surface of a larger drop of water spreads out. Since it is not as curved, it has less magnification than a smaller drop.

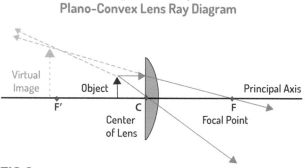

Magnification by
Plano-Convex Lens Ray Diagram

FIG 2

27. Polarized Light

Polarized light consists of light waves vibrating in one direction. **Unpolarized light** consists of light waves that vibrate in different directions. Common examples of unpolarized light are sunlight, light emitted from **incandescent** and **fluorescent** light bulbs, and light from candle flames. Unpolarized light can be transformed into polarized light through a process called light **polarization**, which is a separation of light vibrating in different planes.

People buy sunglasses with **polarized lenses** to reduce glare. When sunlight, which is unpolarized light, reflects off of horizontal surfaces, such as snow or water, the reflected light (glare) is horizontally polarized. Polarized glasses are vertically polarized so as to block horizontally polarized glare. These products are made of a type of specialized plastic in which the molecules are organized in long chains, lined up parallel to each other. This forms a series of slits. Only light waves vibrating in the same direction as these molecules can pass through the slits while others are blocked. Figure 1

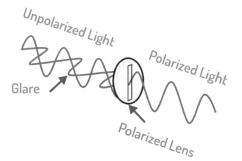

FIG 1

shows the polarization of unpolarized light. Note that there are many light waves in unpolarized light, but Figure 1 is simplified, showing only two waves with one of them passing through and the other one block. If two pairs of polarized lenses are used, the light entering the first lens can be totally blocked by rotating the second lens.

See for Yourself

Materials

2 pairs of polarized sunglasses or two polarizing filters

What to Do

1. Put one pair of glasses on.
2. Observe how objects around you appear.
3. Hold the second pair of glasses in front of your eyes (Figure 2).
4. Slowly rotate the pair of glasses you are holding so that one of the lenses turns in front of your right eye.
5. Observe the quality of vision as you turn the glasses.

What Happened?

One pair of polarized sunglasses cuts down on glare and changes the shade of objects while allowing objects on the other side of the lenses to be viewed. During the rotation of the second pair of glasses, the objects viewed through the right eye got darker until finally nothing could be seen through the combination of the two lenses. This is because the first lens polarized the light by allowing only light waves vibrating in one plane to pass through. The second lens, with slits turned in the opposite direction, blocks this polarized light as shown in Figure 3.

94

FIG 2

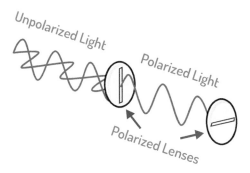

Unpolarized Light

Polarized Light

Polarized Lenses

FIG 3

95

28. Filters

In reference to light, **filters** are transparent materials that allow only some wavelengths of light to transmit, or pass, while absorbing all the others. White light passing through the filter contains all the wavelengths of the visible color spectrum. A red filter appears red to the human eye because it reflects red light. Also, a red filter allows red light to pass through. A red transparent vinyl folder can be used as a filter. Interestingly, these folders appear red, but they are generally not pure red. The red you see is likely a blend of orange, yellow, and red. Figure 1 shows how the folder filters out some light and allows other light to pass through.

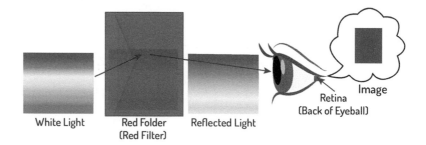

White Light   Red Folder   Reflected Light   Retina   Image
(Red Filter)   (Back of Eyeball)

FIG 1

A filter will allow certain colors to pass through, and words written in the same colors will seem to magically disappear when the filter is placed over the colored writing.

See for Yourself

Materials

colored pencils and/or crayons, yellow, orange, red, blue, green (use as many different shades of each color as possible)

sheet of white paper

red transparent vinyl folder

What to Do

1. Make colored marks on the paper with each colored pencil and/or crayon.
2. Place the sheet of paper with the colored marks inside the red folder.
3. Look at the marks through the red plastic folder and identify the colors that seem to disappear.
4. Make a chart listing the colors that are not visible when viewed through the red plastic.
5. Write a secret message with the colors on the chart that cannot be seen through the red plastic filter (Figure 2).

What Happened?

Placing the folder on top of the colored writing only allows part of the white light to pass through the folder. This light is reflected from letters written in the same color but is absorbed by all other colors. The colored letters that absorb the light appear darker while the colored letters

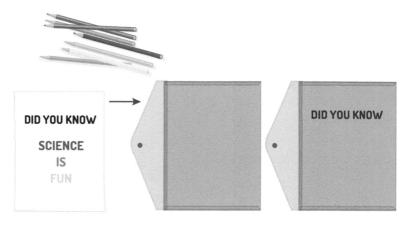

FIG 2

that reflect the light seem to magically disappear. This is because the light waves from some colors blend in with the reflected waves.

29. Optical Density

Optical density has to do with the length of time between the light being absorbed and re-emitted by particles in the medium the light is passing through. The longer this length of time, the more optically dense is the material. It is important not to confuse this term with physical density, which means more particles per volume.

In a vacuum, light waves, electromagnetic waves, travel at a speed of 670,000,000 m/hr (300,000,000 m/s). When light waves hit atoms in a medium, the wave energy is absorbed and electrons in the atoms begin to vibrate. If the frequency of the light wave does not match the natural vibrating frequency of the electrons, the energy is re-emitted in the form of electromagnetic waves. This new light wave has the same frequency and speed as the light rays that were first absorbed. This new wave of light travels at the speed of light in a vacuum through the space between atoms until it hits another atom and the absorption and re-emitting of the light is repeated. This continues until the light exits the medium. Even though the speed of light never changes, the average speed of light through optically dense mediums is slower. The speed of light in an optically dense medium can be compared to a relay race where one runner races a distance and then hands the baton to another runner (Figure 1). This runner repeats the action until the last runner crosses the finish line. If one runner had run the race without stopping, it would have taken less time to finish. But passing the baton from one runner to another increased the time to complete the race, just like the absorption and re-emitting of light by the atoms in an optically dense medium.

FIG 1

See for Yourself

Materials
yardstick (meter stick)
4 helpers
timer
3 pencils

What to Do
1. Outdoors, mark off a racing track of 16 feet (4.8 m). Lay a pencil at the start and the finish line.
2. Assign one helper to be the timekeeper for the race.

3. Stand at the starting line. When the timekeeper says, "One, two, three, go!" start walking at your normal speed to the finish line. The timer will record the time it took you to walk 16 feet (4.8 m).

4. Stand at the starting line again, but this time hold the remaining pencil in your hand with three helpers positioned at 4 foot (1.2 m) intervals along the track (Figure 2).

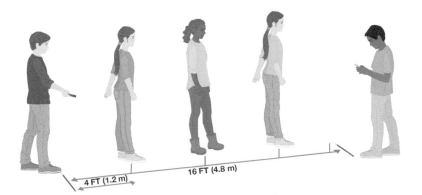

4 FT (1.2 m)   16 FT (4.8 m)

FIG 2

5. The timekeeper will start the timer and stop it when the last walker crosses the finish line.

6. As before, start walking when the timekeeper says, "One, two, three, go!" Walk and hand off the pencil to the next racer who starts walking and hands off the pencil to the next racer. The last racer will receive the pencil and walk across the finish line.

7. Compare the time for the two races. You could also calculate the average speed for each race using this equation:

$$speed = distance / time$$

What Happened?

The time recorded to walk from the starting line to the finish line was less than the time it took to pass the pencil from one person to the next and complete the relay. This activity is not illustrative of how light rays are received and re-emitted by atoms, but it does demonstrate that stopping and starting increases travel time. Therefore, it can be stated that the greater the optical density of a material, the slower the speed of light passing through the material.

30. Refractive Index

Refractive index is a reference to the speed of light in a medium. In equations, the symbol for refractive index is the letter *n*. The higher the refractive index for a material, the more optically dense it is, therefore, the slower the speed light travels through it. Figure 1 is a ray diagram showing the movement of light from air into water, and then back into air. The optical density of water is *n* = 1.3 and for air, *n* = 1. Since the optical density of water is greater than that of air, the speed of light will be slower through water than it is in air. Light refracts when it changes from one medium to another with different optical densities. In Figure 1, a line perpendicular to the surface of the medium is drawn where the light ray enters and exits

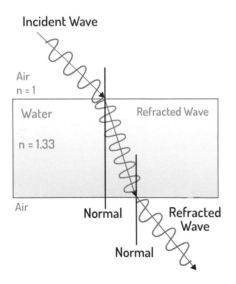

FIG 1

the water. This line is called the **normal**. Note that the light ray refracted toward the normal when it slowed, and the light ray refracted away from the normal when the light ray speeded up. Light rays perpendicular to the surface of a medium pass through with no change in direction. A light ray refracts when **oblique**, at an angle, to the surface of the medium it is entering.

Light rays reflecting off of objects submerged in water will refract at the boundary between the water and air. Your eye receives this refracted light and sends the message to your brain. In the following activity, the messages received by your brain are interpreted as if the coin is floating in the water. It looks like magic, but it's really science.

See for Yourself

Materials
small, shallow, opaque bowl
modeling clay, grape-sized amount
coin, a penny works well
water
helper

What to Do
1. Place the bowl on a table.
2. Use a small piece of clay to secure a coin inside the bowl on the bottom. The coin should be centered.
3. Ask your helper to stand straight up next to the table in front of the bowl.
4. Move the bowl slowly forward until your helper can see the coin (top of Figure 2). Instruct your helper, while standing upright with the coin in view, to slowly take

small steps backward until the coin is barely out of view (bottom of Figure 2), but can still be seen if your helper leans forward.

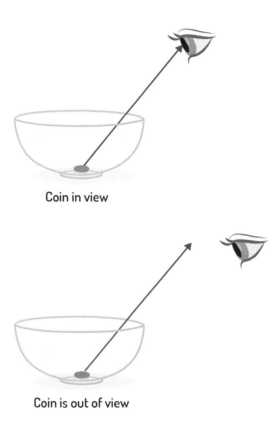

Coin in view

Coin is out of view

FIG 2

5. While your helper is standing upright, with the coin just out of view, slowly pour water into the bowl. Instruct your helper to tell you when the coin comes into view (Figure 3).

FIG 3

What Happened?

Light rays reflected from the coin in the empty bowl move through the air in different directions. Your helper was able to view the coin when reflected light from the coin entered their eyes. The coin is out of sight when light rays from the coin directed toward the eye are blocked by the side of the bowl. Adding water to the bowl changes the direction of the light reflecting off of the coin. The light was refracted when it stopped traveling at a certain speed through the water and traveled at a new speed through a different medium, the air. If your helper is in a position for these refracted light rays to enter their eyes, a virtual image of the coin will appear. Although virtual images look real, they are actually the result of your brain's interpretation of information sent by your eyes. In this case, light from the real coin refracted, changed direction. When going from water into air, your brain interprets light as traveling in straight lines, thus your brain perceives the light as coming from a different location other than where the coin is actually located. The floating coin that you thought you saw was an optical illusion. An **optical illusion** is a perception by the brain that doesn't match what is real. You know that the coin is not really floating, but your brain perceives it to be.

31. Shadows

A shadow is a dark area on the side of an object opposite the light source. A shadow forms when light is blocked by an object. When an object is opaque, meaning light cannot pass through it, a shadow is formed as shown in Figure 1. Shadows confirm that light travels in a straight line. Galileo Galilei (1564–1642), an Italian astronomer, used the Earth's shadow during a lunar eclipse to confirm that the Earth is round. A **lunar eclipse** occurs when the Moon is full and moves into Earth's shadow. In the following activity, you will make a model of the Earth, Moon, and Sun using a white paper circle for the Moon, a polystyrene ball for the Earth, and a flashlight for the Sun. Just like Galileo over 300 years ago, you will note the shadows made by light to make scientific observations.

FIG 1

See for Yourself

Materials

drawing compass

white paper

scissors

tape

2 pencils

ruler

polystyrene ball (3 inches (7.5 cm) in diameter)

modeling clay (golf-ball size)

flashlight

helper

What to Do

1. Use the compass to draw a circle with a diameter of 2 inches (5 cm).
2. Cut out the circle and secure it with tape to one end of a ruler.
3. Insert about 1 inch (2.5 cm) of the second pencil into the polystyrene ball. Use the clay to stand the pencil upright on a flat surface near a wall.
4. Hold the flashlight so it is facing both the ball on the pencil and the wall. Darken the room. Turn the flashlight on and ask your helper to shine the light on the ball. Move the position of the light and/or ball until the darkest round shadow of the ball is formed on the wall.

5. Holding the ruler attached to the white circle, starting on the right side of the shadow, slowly move the circle across the shadow.

6. Observe the changes of the shape of the lighted part of the white paper circle.

FIG 2

What Happened?

The polystyrene ball modeled the Earth, the white paper circle modeled the Moon, and the flashlight modeled the Sun. The Moon moves in its orbit around Earth. During a lunar eclipse, the Moon moves through the Earth's shadow, and the Moon is eclipsed by the shadow. **Eclipse** is the blocking of the light on one celestial body by the moving of another between it and the observer or between it and its source of illumination. The Earth casts a circular shadow. Thus, this shadow's edge is curved as it moves across a full Moon during a lunar eclipse. Galileo used this evidence to confirm that the Earth is a sphere and not a flat surface. Others before Galileo had also collected evidence to support this fact. While previous information was mostly mathematical, Galileo added physical evidence as proof.

II
Force and Motion Introduction

Gravity is the gravitational force that occurs between massive bodies. Gravity is the force acting to pull objects toward Earth's center, and it is perpendicular to Earth's surface. The force of gravity is equal to the weight of an object.

Weight is equal to the gravitational force acting on an object. $F_{wt} = m \times g$; F_{wt} (force of gravity); m (mass of object); g (acceleration due to gravity).

The gravitational field is the area around a massive body, such as Earth, that extends into space, producing a gravitational force on other bodies within this field.

Gravitational field strength at the surface of Earth is 9.8 N/kg. This means an object with a mass of 1 kilogram would be attracted toward Earth's center by a force of 9.8 **newtons**, which is the weight of the object. Thus, the force of gravity on an object within Earth's gravitational field is equal to the weight of the object.

Acceleration of gravity (g) is the acceleration of an object due to the force of gravity. The numerical value of **Earth's acceleration of gravity** is 32 feet/second^2 (9.8 m/second^2).

Freefalling is when an object is dropped with gravity being the only force acting on it. The term "freefalling" is often used more loosely as being an object that is dropped from an elevated height as opposed to being thrown.

The gravitational acceleration of freefalling objects is 32 feet/second ^{2} (9.8 m/second^2), which means the speed of the object increases by 32 feet per second every second (9.8 m/second every second). **Air resistance** is an opposing force against the motion of objects moving through the air. Air resistance has more effect on some things than on others. It depends on the momentum of the object. **Momentum** is the resistance a moving object has to being stopped. Momentum is calculated by this equation:

$$momentum = mass \times velocity$$

An object with greater mass will have more momentum as it falls, and air resistance will have less effect on it.

32. Inertia: Newton's First Law of Motion

Sir Isaac Newton (1642–1726), an English scientist, is the author of three laws describing the relationship between force and motion. **Laws** are descriptions, often mathematical descriptions, of natural phenomena believed to happen the same way every time. A force is a push or a pull on an object.

Newton's First Law of Motion describes the inertia of an object. **Inertia** is the resistance an object has to any change in motion. If an object is at rest, it will remain at rest unless an outside force acts upon it. If an object is in motion, it will remain in motion unless an unbalanced force acts upon it. As the mass of an object increases, the greater is its inertia and the more force is needed to change its state of motion.

See for Yourself

Materials
drinking glass
index card
coin or metal washer

What to Do
1. Place the index card over the mouth of the glass.
2. Position the coin on top of the card so that it is centered over the glass.
3. Quickly and forcefully thump, or flick, the card straight forward with your finger.

FIG 1

4. Repeat the experiment several times. Observe which side of the coin is facing up when it lands.

What Happened?

Your finger applied an unbalanced force to the card, causing it to rapidly move forward. The card moves so quickly that it translates very little force to the coin. The inertia of the coin

116

keeps the coin in its resting place, but without the support of the card, gravity pulls the coin down into the glass. Gravity is the unbalanced force acting on the coin. However, if the card moves too slowly after being thumped, the card will pull slightly on the coin causing the coin to flip over before landing on the bottom of the glass.

33. Rotational Inertia

Inertia is the tendency of an object to resist a change in its motion. **Rotational inertia** is a measure that represents how difficult it is to start or stop the rotation of an object. Rotational inertia depends on the mass of the object and how this mass is distributed. The farther the mass is from the axis of rotation, the higher the rotational inertia; thus, the harder it is to start it to rotate or to stop its rotation.

Kinetic energy is the energy of moving objects. Objects that rotate have two types of kinetic energy, translational and rotational. Translational kinetic is the energy of an object moving in a straight line and rotational kinetic is the energy of an object moving about an axis. A ball at the top of an inclined ramp has potential energy that is converted to both translational and rotational kinetic energy as it rolls down the inclined plane. The potential energy is not evenly split between these two types of kinetic energy. Instead, rotational inertia determines how potential energy is divided.

The mass and diameter of similar shapes, such as cylinders and spheres, do not determine rotational inertia. Rather, what determines rotational inertia is the distribution of mass. Solid shapes have less rotational inertia than hollow shapes. Thus, when hollow and solid shapes are tested, the solid shape will roll faster because more of the potential energy is converted to translational kinetic energy.

See for Yourself

Materials

card table or another lightweight flat surface
2 books of equal thickness
marble or small solid ball
hollow ball such as a tennis ball, basketball, or volleyball
sealed can with solid food
empty can with both ends removed
helper

What to Do

1. Place one book under each of two legs of a card table so the surface is tilted forming an inclined plane.
2. Hold the marble and hollow ball at the top of the inclined plane formed by the surface of the table.
3. Ask your helper to catch the rolling spheres and confirm which of the two reached the bottom of the incline first. Make note of the winners of each race so that you can list the test materials in order of their translational speed down the incline formed by the raised table.

FIG 1

4. Repeat steps #2 and #3 using the two cans, one full and unopened, the other hollow with both ends open.
5. Repeat steps #2 and #3 twice, first note the two winners, the marble and the solid can of food, and then compare the two losers, the can with open ends and the hollow ball.
6. List the four objects in order of speed down the incline from fastest to slowest.

120

What Happened?

The marble was faster than the hollow ball and the can of food was faster than the hollow can. In both of these two races, the solid objects were faster. This is because the solid objects had a lower rotational inertia than their opponents, meaning more of their potential energy at the top of the ramp was used to accelerate them down the ramp. When compared, the marble was faster than the filled can. This tells you that the rotational inertia of the marble is less than that of the can of food.

The hollow can and hollow ball lost against their opponents who were solid. When these two raced, the hollow ball was faster than the hollow can. Notice that a sphere was the winner again. From these observations, one can conclude that solid objects have less rotational inertia than hollow ones, and spheres have lower rotational inertia than cylinders. The lower the rotational inertia, the faster the speed down an incline. In conclusion, here is a list of the tested objects from fastest to slowest:

solid ball
can of solid food
hollow ball
can with open ends

34. Acceleration

Acceleration is the change of velocity in a specific time period and in a specific direction. **Newton's Second Law of Motion** states that the net force acting on an object is equal to its mass times its acceleration. An equation that compares this relationship is:

$$F_{net}\,(\text{net force}) = m\,(\text{mass}) \times a\,(\text{acceleration})$$

A **net force (F_{net})** is the summation of all forces acting on an object. An example shown in Figure 1 is two people pushing and pulling on a wagon. The net force is the sum total of the forces acting on the wagon. Since both applied forces are in the same direction, the net force on the wagon is 70 N.

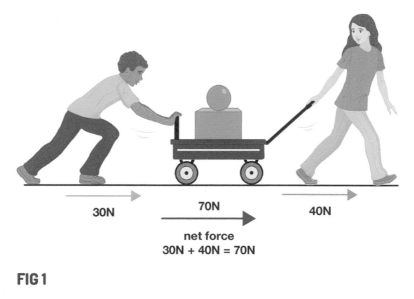

30N   70N   40N

net force
30N + 40N = 70N

FIG 1

Two things that affect the acceleration of the wagon and its contents are the net force acting on it and the total mass of the wagon and its contents. Using the equation for Newton's Second Law of Motion, $F_{net} = ma$, the effect that mass has on acceleration can be determined. If the F_{net} in the equation is not changed, then the mass of an object determines its acceleration. Think about it!

$$F_{net} = \text{mass} \times \text{acceleration}$$

$$70\,N = 35\,kg \times 2\frac{m}{s^2}$$

$$70\,N = 5\,kg \times 14\frac{m}{s^2}$$

When the mass decreases, the acceleration increases and, vice versa, as the mass increases, the acceleration decreases.

See for Yourself

Materials

scissors
ruler with a center groove
paper cup, 8 ounces (236 mL)
book
plain sheet of paper
marble
pencil
clay, golf-ball size

What to Do

1. Cut a 2-inch (5-cm) square section from the top of the paper cup.
2. Lay the book flat on the table and rest one end of the ruler on the book.
3. Place the paper under the end of the ruler and then place the cup on the paper with the cut-out section over the ruler so that the ruler touches the back of the cup.
4. Mark a starting line on the paper next to the cup.
5. Place the marble in the center groove of the ruler at its raised end.
6. Release the marble and mark the position of the cup on the paper (Figure 2). Remove the marble and return the cup to its original position.

FIG 2

7. Place the clay on top of the cup to increase its mass, and then repeat steps #3 to #6. Compare the distance the less massive cup moves with that of the more massive cup.

What Happened?

The acceleration of the stationary cup was zero. When the marble struck the cup, the cup accelerated in the direction that the marble was moving. The same thing occurred after the clay was added to the cup. However, in this case, the clay added mass to the cup, so the same amount of force, applied by the moving marble, could not achieve the same amount of acceleration, thus the cup was not moved as far as the less massive cup. So, if the force applied is the same, an object with less mass will have a greater acceleration than a more massive object.

35. Impulse

Impulse is the force applied to stop a moving object multiplied by the total time the force was applied. Impulse is equal to the change in **momentum** of the moving object. Momentum is a measure of how difficult it is to stop a moving object. This relationship is expressed by the equation (the Greek letter Δ is used in equations to mean a 'change' in something):

$$F(\text{stopping force}) \times \Delta t(\text{change in time})$$
$$= m(\text{mass of object}) \times \Delta v\,(\text{change in velocity})$$

or

$$F \times \Delta t = m \times \Delta v$$

If the moving object is fragile, such as a water balloon, it is less likely to break when being stopped by something like your hand or a towel if its speed is slowly decreased. Thus, increasing the time it takes to stop the object by gradually slowing it down decreases the force needed to stop it. The time of **deceleration** starts when the object is caught and ends when the object is stationary.

See for Yourself

Materials
water balloons
tap water
2 helpers
large bath towel or comparably sized piece of cloth

What to Do

1. Fill four or more balloons with water.
2. Outdoors in an open area, ask both of your helpers to spread the towel to form a loose net as shown in Figure 1.

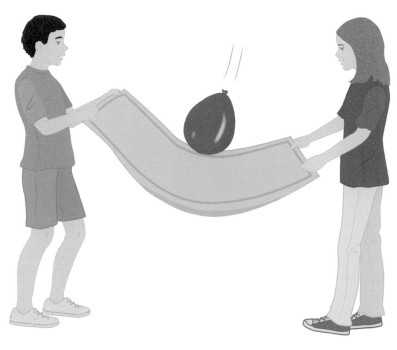

FIG 1

3. Stand next to the towel and hold one of the water balloons. Begin walking away perpendicular from the towel while counting off four large steps. Turn around so that you face the towel.

127

4. Gently toss the water balloon so your helpers will be able to catch it in the towel while attempting not to break the balloon.

5. Take two large steps back and again toss the balloon. Release the balloon gently but with enough speed so that it reaches the towel. Repeat this step several times taking two steps back each trial until the balloon breaks.

6. As you toss the balloon longer distances, observe the movement of the towel when the balloon makes impact.

What Happened?

As the distance from the towel increases, the velocity of the balloon must be increased for the balloon to reach the towel. When the velocity of the balloon increases, its momentum ($m \times v$) increases. Impulse ($F \times \Delta t$) equals change in momentum ($m \times \Delta v$). In order to reduce the amount of force (F) needed to stop the water balloon, the deceleration time must be increased. Remember that $F \times \Delta t = m \times \Delta v$. This means the product of $F \times \Delta t$ equals the product of $m \times \Delta v$.

The towel serves the purpose of allowing the balloon, and the water inside, to slow down at a rate so as not to break the balloon upon impact. As the time to stop the balloon increases, the force needed to stop it decreases. If you understand this principle, you will likely win the next egg toss at your family picnic! What do the contestants do to slow down the rate that the egg is traveling at when it hits their hand? They increase the stopping time by moving their hand fluidly, in the direction that the egg had been traveling, after catching the egg. This allows the egg and the fluid inside to more slowly come to a stop.

36. Gravity

Gravity is the force of attraction between two bodies. The more massive the body, the greater is its gravitational pull. The gravitational attraction between everyday objects is minute in comparison to the attraction between everyday objects and the Earth. Thus, the term gravity generally refers to Earth's gravitational pull unless otherwise specified. Remember, gravity pulls objects toward the center of Earth, which means the direction is perpendicular to Earth's surface. The **weight** of an object is the measure of the force of gravity acting on it. Yes, when you stand on a scale, you are measuring the force of Earth's gravity pulling down on you.

An object dropped from a height, regardless of its mass, will accelerate due to gravity at a rate of 32 ft/s^2 (9.8 m/s^2). While falling through air, the resistance of air can slow the falling acceleration of lightweight objects, but has little effect on heavier objects.

See for Yourself

Materials
2 coins, 1 larger than the other
sheet of paper
pencil
scissors
small towel

What to Do
1. Lay the smaller coin on the paper. Use the pencil to trace around the coin, and then cut out the paper circle.

2. Lay the towel on a table to keep the dropped coin from rolling. Then, about 1 yard (90 cm) above the towel, hold the coin in one hand and the paper circle in your other hand.

3. Drop the coin and paper. Observe how each of them falls through the air.

4. Place the paper circle below the large coin. Hold the pair as shown in Figure 1 so that they are about 1 yard (90 cm) above the towel on the table.

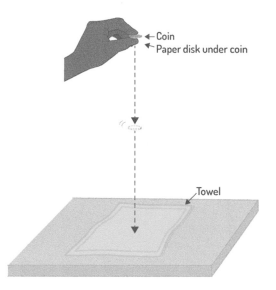

←Coin
←Paper disk under coin

Towel

FIG 1

5. Release and allow the coin and paper to fall. Observe the position of the paper circle relative to the coin as they fall.

130

6. Repeat steps #4, and #5, reversing the position of the paper and coin; place the paper on top of the coin.

What Happened?

When the coin and paper are dropped separately, the coin falls straight down and the paper flutters around in the air before landing.

When the coin and paper are held together with the paper under the coin, they both land at the same time. The coin is more massive; thus, it has more weight than the paper circle.

The heavy coin pushes its way through the air; air resistance has little effect on the coin. The upward force of air on the paper is great enough to slow its descent. The coin is not pushing the paper down, instead the paper and coin are accelerating at the same rate. To confirm this the paper was placed on top of the coin. The results were the same; the coin and paper fell together and landed together. Again, this occurred because the coin had a greater downward force of gravity and pushed the air molecules out of the way, thus forming a clear path through which the paper fell downward to the towel.

37. Friction

Friction is the force that opposes motion between two surfaces in contact with each other. There are four types of friction: fluid, static, sliding, and rolling. **Fluid friction** is the opposition to the motion of objects moving through a fluid, such as air and water.

Static, sliding, and rolling friction occur between solid surfaces. **Static friction** occurs between a stationary object and the surface it rests on. **Sliding friction**, also called **kinetic friction**, occurs when two surfaces in motion rub against each other. Static friction is generally greater than sliding friction when comparing the same two surfaces that are in contact. **Rolling friction** is when an object rolls over a surface. Rolling friction is less than sliding friction.

See for Yourself

Materials
string, 24 inches (60 cm)
rubber band
2 large books
10 round marking pens
ruler

What to Do
1. Stack the books on the table.
2. Tie the string around the bottom book.
3. Attach the string to the rubber band.

4. Move the stack of books by pulling on the rubber band as shown in Figure 1. Make note how far the rubber band had to stretch before the books started moving and again after the books were in motion.

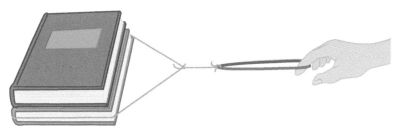

FIG 1

5. Place the 10 marking pens under the stack of books (Figure 2).

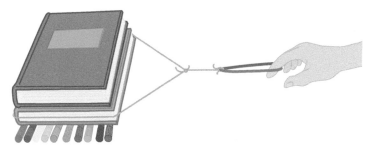

FIG 2

6. Repeat step #4.

What Happened?

The rubber band stretches when trying to start the stack of books with the bottom book sitting flat against the surface of the table. This is because of the static friction between the book and the table's surface. The least force required to move the books was with the round pens under the stack. This is because rolling friction is less than sliding or the static friction acting against the movement of the books.

38. Air Resistance

Air resistance is the fluid friction on objects moving through air. This frictional force is also called **drag force**. The force of gravity accelerates falling objects at a rate of 32 ft/s² (9.8 m/s²). This means their speed increases by 32 ft/s (9.8 m/s) for every second they fall. While air resistance pushes up on objects falling through air, the force of gravity pulls the objects down. The net force of these two forces, which are acting in opposite directions on the falling object, would be less than the force of gravity. Thus, the falling object accelerates more slowly than it would without the air resistance. The greater the air resistance, the slower the acceleration of falling objects

See for Yourself

Materials

3 basket-type coffee filters
helper

What to Do

1. With your hands, flatten one of the coffee filters. Leave the sides of the second coffee filter as vertical as possible.
2. Hold one filter in the palm of each hand (Figure 1). Hold the bowl-shaped filter with its sides pointing up.
3. Raise your hands as high as possible to equal heights, and then release both coffee filters. Observe how the filters fall through the air. Does one reach the floor first?
4. Repeat steps #2 and #3 three or more times and compare the results.

5. Extend this activity by adding a third paper filter, wadded into a very tight ball, and repeating. You will need a helper to drop all of the filter papers from the same height simultaneously.

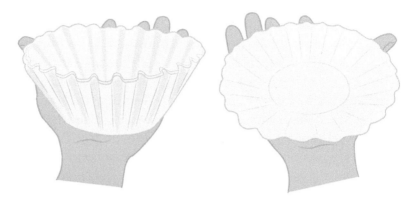

FIG 1

What Happened?

Repeating the process multiple times produced the same results. Flattening the coffee filter increased the surface area of this falling object. The flattened coffee filter had greater air resistance pushing up on the object which caused it to drift downward more slowly. In comparison, the bowl-shaped coffee filter fell faster because it had less air resistance pushing against its bottom surface area than the flattened filter. The smaller the surface area of a falling object, the less air resistance, and the faster the object will accelerate. The wadded coffee filter ball had a smaller surface than the shape of the other two filter papers; thus, it had a faster acceleration.

39. Drag Force

Drag force is a force on an object as it moves through a fluid (gas or liquid). A drag force acts upon the object opposite of the direction it is moving through a fluid; thus, it is a type of friction called **fluid friction**. An example of a drag force is the air resistance pushing on objects moving through air. Air resistance essentially depends on two things: the velocity (speed in a specific direction) of the object and the object's cross-sectional area. Not all falling objects continue to increase in velocity until they hit the ground. Instead, they fall and increase in velocity until the upward drag force of the air equals the downward force of gravity. When these two forces, drag and gravity, are equal, the net force acting on the object is zero, thus the object no longer accelerates. But it does continue to move at a constant velocity toward the ground. The object has reached its **terminal velocity**. Skydivers use parachutes so that, while falling, they will reach a slow terminal velocity. The shape of the parachute serves to increase the cross-sectional area of the falling skydiver, thus increasing the drag force. The larger the area of a parachute, the greater the drag force. This results in the terminal velocity being achieved in a shorter time.

See for Yourself

Materials
scissors
ruler
small plastic garbage bag

string

2 small washers

What to Do

1. Cut a 12-inch (30-cm) square from the plastic bag.
2. Cut eight separate strings of about 20 inches (50 cm) long.
3. Tie a string to each corner of the plastic square.
4. Tie the four free ends of the strings together in a knot. Be sure the strings are all the same length.
5. Use a string about 4 inches (10 cm) long to attach a washer to the knot in the parachute strings (Figure 1).

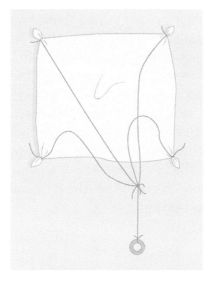

FIG 1

6. Make a larger parachute using a 24-inch (60-cm) square of plastic and the four remaining strings.

138

7. Attach a washer to the parachute with a 4-inch (10-cm) piece of string as before.

8. Prepare the parachutes for a test flight using these steps:
- Place the four ends of each parachute together.
- Flatten the plastic and fold in half, top to bottom.
- Loosely wrap the string around the folded plastic.

9. Throw the parachutes up into the air one at a time, or find a safe place from which to drop the parachutes, and observe the time it takes for each to reach the ground (Figure 2).

FIG 2

What Happened?

The larger parachute opens and floats to the ground more slowly than the smaller parachute. This is because the larger the area of the parachute, the greater the drag created on the parachute. Remember, since both parachutes have objects of equal weight attached and the difference in the weight of the parachute is negligible, the force of gravity acting on each parachute is the same. It took longer for the smaller parachute to reach terminal velocity and, depending on the height from which it was dropped, it may not have had enough time to reach terminal velocity. Whereas the parachute with the larger area reached terminal velocity quickly and slowly floated down.

40. Air Pressure

Pressure is a measurement of force on an area. Pressure is measured in pounds per square inch, psi (pascals, Pa, or newtons per square meter). Air pressure is the measure of the weight of air above a specific area. Figure 1 represents an area 1 inch (2.5 cm) square. Imagine a cubic column of air above this square that reaches to the top of Earth's atmosphere. The column contains air molecules. The weight of all these air molecules is about 14.7 pounds (65.4 N), and this weight is pushing down on the 1 inch (2.5 cm) square area.

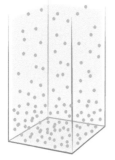

Air
Pressure

1 inch surface area

FIG 1

As air is heated, the molecules move faster and farther apart. With fewer air molecules in the column in Figure 1, the weight of the air pushing on the 1 inch (2.5 cm) square area would be less than if the molecules were cooler and closer together. The unequal heating of Earth's surface,

141

water, and soil causes changes in the air pressure over different regions. Air and other fluids move from high-pressure areas to low-pressure areas. This movement of air is called **wind**. Air pressure changes as the **density** of air molecules above a surface changes. Based on these principles, the air pressure inside a container can be increased by increasing the number of air molecules within the container.

See for Yourself

Materials

empty narrow-necked water bottle or soda bottle
sheet of notebook paper

What to Do

1. Lay the empty bottle on its side with its mouth at the edge of the table.
2. Tear off about a 1 inch (2.5 cm) square from the paper. Roll the paper into a tight wad shaped like a ball.
3. Rest the wad of paper just inside the opening of the bottle's neck.

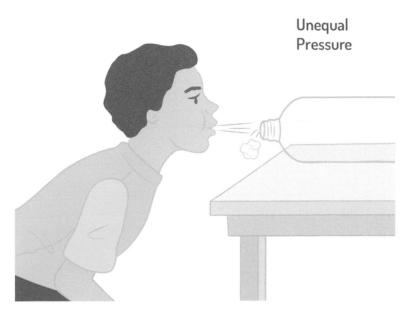

Unequal
Pressure

FIG 2

4. Put your mouth level with the neck of the bottle and try
   to blow the paper wad into the bottle (Figure 2).
5. Repeat this experiment to make sure you get the
   same results.

What Happened?

Blowing into the bottle causes the wad of paper to fly out.
Before you blew into the bottle, the amount of air inside and
outside the bottle was the same, so the air pressure inside
and outside the bottle was equal. Blowing into the bottle

increased the amount of air, thus increasing the air pressure inside the bottle. Air moves from a high-pressure area to a low-pressure area. Just like in nature, this movement of air molecules creates wind. This gust of wind, caused by air rushing out of the bottle, carried the paper wad forward and out of the neck of the bottle.

41. Torque

Torque is a **turning force** that causes **rotation**, which is movement around an axis or center point, such as the axle on a car around which the wheel turns. People sitting on the ends of a seesaw are applying torque, which causes the ends of the seesaw to rotate. The point of rotation is called the **pivot point**, which is the center support of the seesaw. When the torque applied to each end of the seesaw is equal, the seesaw will balance, meaning it will be horizontal. Torque can be calculated by this equation: $T = F \times d$. This is read as torque equals the force applied times the distance of the applied force from the pivot. Torque is measured in **newton-meters** (Nm). A beam that is supported at its center can be used to demonstrate torque.

See for Yourself

Materials
string 30 inches (75 cm)
ruler with holes for a three-ring binder
tape
3 clothespins

What to Do
1. Thread the string through the center hole of the ruler and then tape the ends of the string to the edge of a table.
2. Clip one clothespin the same distance from each end of the ruler. The ruler should be as horizontal as possible, meaning it should be balanced. If the ruler dips down lower on one side, move the clothespin at the lower end a small distance at a time toward the center until the ruler is balanced (Figure 1).

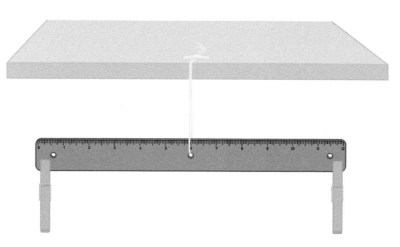

FIG 1

3. Clip a second clothespin to the bottom of a clothespin. Now move the two combined clothespins a small distance at a time closer to the center until the ruler is again balanced. Look at the ruler and compare the distance from its center to each of the clothespins (Figure 2).

What Happened?

The ruler acts as a beam. The balance beam in this activity has a hole in its center that acts as the pivot point with a string supporting it. The clothespins are placed so that the torque applied to each end is equal; thus, the ruler balances.

Two combined clothespins double the torque on one end so that the end of the ruler swings down in a counterclockwise direction. This action raises the opposite end, which has less torque. Instead of adding a second clothespin to equalize the torque, the two clothespins were moved closer to the pivot point until the torque produced was

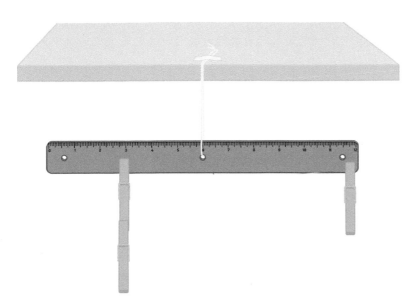

FIG 2

equal to the torque produced by a single clothespin on the other end.

The distance from the pivot for the two combined clothespins should be close to half the distance for the single clothespin. The measurements are not exact because it is difficult to balance the ruler due to variables such as the mass of each clothespin, table vibrations, or even the air movement around the ruler.

42. Resultant Force of Gravity

Weight (F_{wt}) is the **resultant force** of **gravity**, which is the sum of all the forces of gravity acting on every part of an object. Every atom that makes up an object is subject to the pull of Earth's gravitational force. If not bound together, the atoms in a solid would individually fall, but they are linked together to form the object and give it a distinct shape. In Figure 1, an object is suspended on a spring scale that measures weight. This weight represents the single force, or resultant force, representing the sum of the force of gravity acting on every atom in the object simultaneously. This resultant force (R),

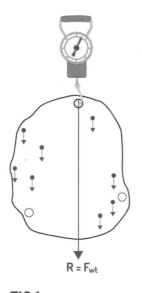

$R = F_{wt}$

FIG 1

is also called force weight (F_{wt}) No matter how an object is suspended from a spring scale, the resultant force will remain the same.

See for Yourself

Materials

spring scale
shoe

What to Do

1. Hook the spring scale to the shoe and record the weight of the shoe.
2. Repeat step #1, hooking the spring scale to another place on the shoe. To further confirm your results, you can hook the spring scale to more places on the shoe.
3. Compare the different weight measurements.

What Happened?

The weight of the shoe is the same regardless of how it was hung from the scale. The measurement of the shoe's weight is the resultant force of gravity acting on all the molecules making up the shoe.

FIG 2

150

43. Center of Gravity

The **center of gravity** is the point upon which the weight of an object or **system** (combination of objects working as a unit) may be considered to act. This weight is the resultant force of gravity pulling down on every particle making up the object. When an object is freely suspended, its center of gravity is always located on a line below the point of suspension. To discover the center of gravity, one can draw several lines, each from a different point of suspension. Where the lines cross is the center of gravity of the object.

See for Yourself

Materials

cardstock, paper plate, or thin cardboard at least 6 inches (15 cm) square

scissors

paper hole punch

string, 12 inches (30 cm)

metal paper clip

metal washer

pencil

helper

What to Do

1. Draw an irregular shape on the cardstock and cut out the shape.
2. Use the paper hole punch to make two holes around the edge of the paper. Do not place the holes directly across from each other and space them out.

151

3. Tie one end of the string to a paper clip and the free end to a washer. Bend the end of the paperclip out to form a hook. This is a plumb bob.
4. Insert the hook of the plumb bob in one of the holes in the paper.
5. Hold the top of the paperclip hook so that the paper and plumb bob swing freely.
6. When the paper and plumb bob are stationary, hold the string taut while your helper draws a line next to the string.
7. Repeat steps #4, #5, and #6 using the other hole in the paper.

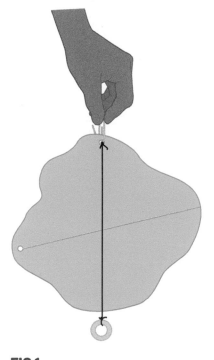

FIG 1

What Happened?

The **plumb bob** is free to swing, but gravity pulls it straight down. When the pump bob is hung in each hole, tracing the line of the string shows the direction of the gravitational pull on the paper. The two lines drawn on the paper cross at the paper's center of gravity. An object can be balanced by supporting it at its center of gravity. If you support the paper where the two lines cross, the paper can be balanced as shown in Figure 2.

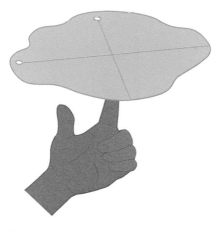

FIG 2

153

44. Balance

Balance occurs when an object or system is supported at its center of gravity. A system is composed of connected parts. An object is said to be balanced when the torque on each side of the center of gravity is equal. An object or system can be balanced if supported at its center of gravity.

See for Yourself

Materials

2 metal forks
drinking glass or wide-mouthed glass jar (do not use plastic)
modeling clay
round wooden toothpick
adult helper (optional)

What to Do

1. Make a ball of clay about the size of a large marble.
2. Insert the tip of one of the forks into the clay ball.
3. Insert the second fork at about a 45° angle from the first fork.
4. Insert one end of the toothpick in the clay between the forks.
5. Lay the toothpick on the edge of the glass as shown in Figure 1. Gently adjust the toothpick on the edge of the glass by sliding it backward or forward slowly until the clay–forks system balances.

Note: If the system is difficult to balance, change the angle of the forks.

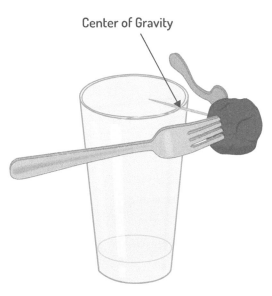

Center of Gravity

FIG 1

What Happened?

There is one point, which can be located on the toothpick, that will support the weight of both forks and the clay. This point is the center of gravity. This is possible when the angle of the forks is such that their weight plus the weight of the clay is distributed so the center of gravity for this system is a point on the toothpick. Note that this system starts at the edge of the glass rim. In other words, the part of the toothpick extending into the glass is useless. If you ask an adult to set the end of the toothpick extending into the glass on fire you will see that the toothpick will burn up to the edge of the glass and stop. The fire stops because it requires **heat** for the wood to burn and the glass absorbs enough heat to extinguish the fire. The clay–forks system remains balanced on the tiny part of the toothpick touching the glass rim.

45. Shifting the Center of Gravity

The center of gravity of an object, such as the ruler in Figure 1, is the point where the resultant force of gravity appears to be. This means that the object can be balanced if supported at this point. Figure 1 shows that the total of the gravitational forces acting on all the atoms on each side of the center of gravity produce the same torque. The torque pulling down on one side tends to cause a clockwise rotation, which on the opposite side the rotation would be counterclockwise. Thus, the ruler is balanced when supported at its center of gravity, which is at the 6 inch (15 cm) mark.

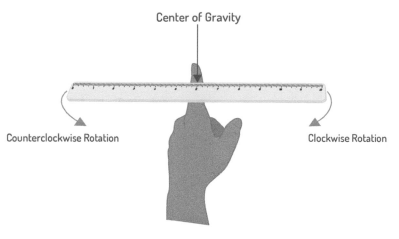

Center of Gravity

Counterclockwise Rotation

Clockwise Rotation

FIG 1

If the ruler is placed on a table, the most that can be extended over the edge of the table is 6 inches (15 cm). But, if a weight is placed on the end of the ruler as shown in Figure 2, the center of gravity (CG) of the system is closer to the weight and is identified in the figure as being at 8 inches (20 cm). This means that up to, but not more than, 8 inches (20) can extend over the table's edge without the ruler rotating about the pivot or point of support in a counterclockwise direction.

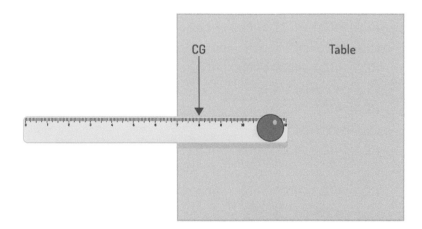

FIG 2

As long as the center of gravity of an object or system is being supported, the object is stable and will not rotate around its center of gravity, which is the pivot.

158

See for Yourself

Materials

wooden ruler
string, 12 inches (30 cm)
hammer
helper

What to Do

1. Lay the ruler flat on a table with about 6 inches (15 cm) extending over the table's edge.
2. Tie the ends of the string together to form a loop.
3. Insert the handle of the hammer in the loop.
4. Using Figure 3 as a guide, position the hammer in the string loop so that the handle end of the hammer rests against the ruler.

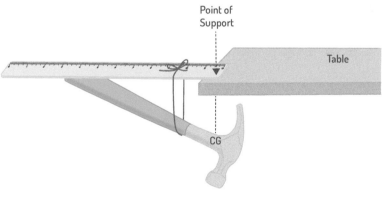

Point of Support

Table

CG

FIG 3

5. Slowly nudge the zero end of the ruler closer to the edge of the table. Adjust the position of the hammer and/or the string so that only a small tip of the ruler is being supported by the table.

What Happened?

Like the ruler in Figure 2, when weight is added to one end of the ruler the result is a shift in the center of gravity. In this activity, the ruler is part of a system in which a string is used to position the hammer so that its weight increases the torque producing a clockwise rotation around the pivot point or point of support, which is the edge of the table. As long as the center of gravity of the system is being supported, the ruler and hammer balance. Yes, it looks like magic, but you now know it is all about physics. Mobiles are another example of placing weights so that the system is balanced at its center of gravity.

46. Action/Reaction

Newton's Third Law of Motion is often referred to as action and reaction forces. This law basically describes the force each object applies to the other when the two are in contact with each other.

FIG 1

For example, when a baseball and bat simultaneously come together, as in Figure 1, the amount of force the bat applies to the ball is the same as the force the ball applies on the bat. Remember, that one force is not applied first. In fact, they occur simultaneously.

The two pairs of forces are equal and act in the opposite direction, but do not act on the same object. The pair of forces in Figure 1 can be stated like this:

161

The ball pushes the bat in one direction.

The bat pushes with the same force on the ball in the opposite direction.

Any time there is an interaction between two objects, there are action and reaction forces.

See for Yourself

Materials
sturdy cardboard
rubber band
scissors
container of water at least 4 inches (10 cm) deep
ruler

What to Do
1. Cut a 4 inch (10 cm) square from the cardboard.
2. Shape the boat by cutting one side into a point and cutting out a 2 inch (5 cm) square from the opposite end.
3. Loop the rubber band over the ends of the boat (Figure 2).
4. Cut a paddle from the cardboard. Make it 1 inch × 2 inches (2.5 cm × 5 cm). Insert the paddle between the sides of the rubber band.
5. From the back of the boat, turn the cardboard paddle toward you to wind the rubber band.
6. Place the boat in the container of water and release the paddle. Observe both the direction in which the paddle is turning and the direction in which the boat is moving through the water (Figure 3).
7. Repeat steps #5 and #6 winding the rubber band in the opposite direction.

162

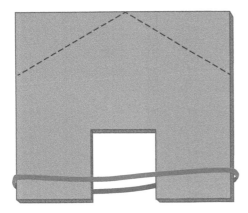

FIG 2

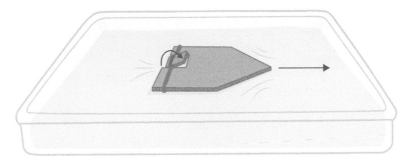

FIG 3

What Happened?

Your muscles are working when you wind up the rubber band. Thus, the twisted rubber band and paddle have stored energy, called potential energy (PE). When the twisted rubber band is released, it unwinds and the paddle turns. The stored potential energy is transferred to kinetic

163

energy (KE), which is energy of a moving object. The paddle pushed on the water and the water pushed on the paddle. The two pairs of forces are equal and act in the opposite direction, but do not act on the same object. The pair of forces can be stated like this:

- The paddle pushes the water in one direction.
- The water pushes with the same force on the paddle in the opposite direction.

Remember that the paddle is part of the boat; thus, pushing on the paddle causes the boat to move. This experiment demonstrates Newton's Third Law of Motion, which is often referred to as action/reaction forces.

47. Normal Force

Normal, in the study of mathematics, is another name for perpendicular. A **normal force** is a perpendicular force of one object acting on the surface of another object. The two objects must be in contact with each other. According to Newton's Third Law of Motion, a bowling ball sitting on a table pushes down on the table's surface and the table pushes up on the ball with an equal amount of force.

Gravity pulls objects downward toward the center of the Earth, so it makes sense that the ball pushes down on the table. But, how can an inanimate object, such as a table, push up on the ball? Also, how does the table know to push with a force equal to the weight of the ball? The table can't think. Instead, imagine the molecules in the table's surface squeezing together as the ball presses down on them. In Figure 1, a model represents how compressed molecules behave as if tiny springs connect them. As the ball pushes down, it squeezes the molecules together until the upward force of these springs is equal to the weight of the ball. When the ball is removed, the molecules return to their normal position. The model in Figure 1 only shows the molecules in the table, but the molecules in the surface of the ball are also compressed in response to the force of the table on the ball.

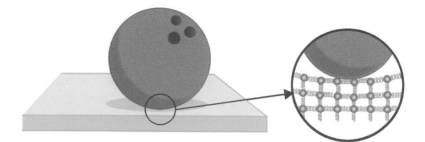

FIG 1

The stronger the "springs" in the surface supporting the ball, the less the surface will sag.

See for Yourself

Material
scissors
3 balloons, 9 inches (23 cm) round
wide-mouth glass or jar
small paper cup, 3 ounces (89 mL)
coins or metal washers

What to Do
1. Cut the upper portion (the part with the opening) off of each balloon. Keep the bottom sections.
2. Stretch the bottom of one balloon over the mouth of the glass. Observe the surface of the stretched rubber.
3. Set the paper cup in the center of the stretched balloon.
4. Add coins to the cup until the rubber surface curves down due to the weight of the cup of coins (Figure 2). Make note of how much the surface sags.

166

FIG 2   **FIG 3**

5. Remove the cup and stretch a second balloon bottom over the first one.
6. Set the cup of coins in the center of the stretched balloon (Figure 3). Again, make note of how much the surface sags now with a double layer of rubber.
7. Repeat steps #5 and #6 using the remaining balloon bottom.

What Happened?

The weight of the cup of coins on the stretched rubber caused the surface of the rubber to sag. This happened because the weight pushed the rubber molecules down-ward. The rubber molecules are squeezed downward. This movement applies a normal force to the cup equal to the weight of the cup. In this case, the compressed molecules do not return to their normal position, resulting in the surface sagging beneath the weight. As each layer of rubber is added, the surface of the rubber sags less and less. The multiple layers of rubber respond to the weight of the cup more like the surface of a solid table. In conclusion, it can be observed that the normal force of the rubber surface will equal the normal force weight of the cup of coins.

48. Balloon Rocket

A balloon rocket is a rubber balloon filled with air that moves when propelled by pressure. While the air leaving the balloon is traveling in one direction, the balloon rocket travels in the opposite direction. Newton's Third Law of Motion states that for every action there is an equal and opposite reaction. This is called action/reaction forces. Newton's Third Law of Motion is describing a pair of equal forces, pushing on two different surfaces in opposite directions. When the air escapes through the mouth of the balloon, the balloon pushes the air out and the air inside pushes the balloon in the opposite direction. In Figure 1, a "balloon rocket" is the

FIG 1

source of **thrust**, a force that pushes the car forward. Thus, a pair of action/reaction forces not only move the balloon vehicle, but also describe why a rocket in outer space can blast off.

See for Yourself

Materials

modeling clay, golf-ball size
dowel rods ¼ inch × 36 inches (0.63 cm × 90 cm)
balloon, long
cellophane tape
drinking straw, straight
helper

What to Do

1. On an outdoor solid surface such as a table in a clear area, use the clay to stand the dowel rod vertically.
2. Inflate the balloon and twist the opening several times to close it.
3. While holding the balloon closed, ask a helper to tape the straw to the middle of the balloon; slide the straw over the dowel rod so that the balloon rests at the bottom of the rod.
4. Release the balloon and observe its motion (Figure 2).

What Happened?

As the balloon deflates, it moves up the dowel and into the air. The attached straw is directing the flight upwards and the straw remains attached to the balloon during its flight.

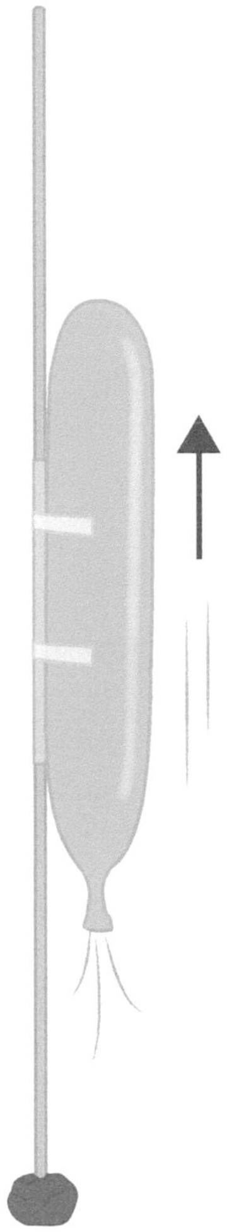

FIG 2

The air inside the balloon is escaping in one direction causing the balloon to move in the opposite direction. We can compare the physics behind the motion of the balloon rocket to the motion of rockets in space. A rocket, whether it's a balloon rocket on Earth or a lunar module blasting off the Moon's surface are not propelled because the escaping gas pushes on air, with the air pushing back. Newton's Third Law of Motion explains both the movement of the balloon rocket as well as the lunar module. Air inside the balloon is pushing out on every area of the balloon. At the same time, the inside surface of the balloon is pushing in on the air inside. Balloon A in Figure 3 represents only a small portion of action/reaction pairs. These forces are described as follows:

- The air inside the balloon pushes out on the inside surface of the balloon.
- The inside surface of the balloon pushes in on the air inside the balloon.

Balloon B represents only two sets of action/reaction pairs and they are in line with the mouth of the balloon. Balloon C is open; thus, the pair of forces at the bottom of the balloon and directions above the opening are no longer there. While the balloon remains closed, there is no motion, but when the

171

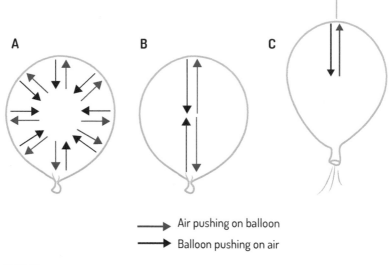

A B C

→ Air pushing on balloon
→ Balloon pushing on air

FIG 3

mouth of the balloon is opened, one of the pairs of forces disappears. The remaining pair of forces in balloon C are representative of all the acting forces inside the balloon. The balloon contracts and squeezes the air out the opening while the air continues to push outward. Thus, air is pushed out by the balloon and the balloon is pushed forward by the force of the air acting on it.

49. Bounce

Bounce is to rebound, or spring back after hitting a surface, such as the basketball in Figure 1.

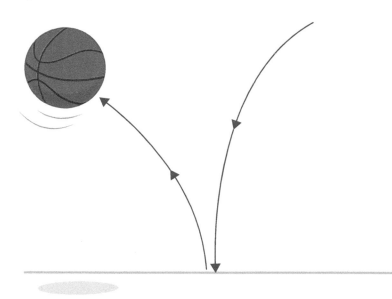

FIG 1

Balls with hollow centers are filled with air, which is a gas. All gases are in constant motion and air inside a ball is continuously bouncing off of the inside surfaces of the ball. When heated, gases move faster and the molecules of gas move farther apart, so the space they occupy becomes larger: it expands. With more kinetic energy, heated air has a higher pressure inside a ball. When cooled, the reverse happens and the gas molecules move slower and come

173

closer together, so the space they occupy contracts. Having less kinetic energy, cooled air has a lower pressure inside the ball.

When a bouncing ball hits the floor, it applies a force to the floor, and in response the floor applies an equal but opposite force to the ball. As the bottom of the ball is pressed upward by the floor, the bottom is being pushed inward. The reduced volume inside the ball compresses the air, raising the pressure, and ultimately resulting in the air pushing the ball back to its original shape. The air returns to its previous volume and pressure. In the process, the ball bounces upward. Primarily, the height of the bounce will depend on the pressure of the air inside the ball. The higher the pressure, the higher the bounce.

See for Yourself

Materials

tennis ball
yardstick (meter stick)
refrigerator with freezer or ice in a cooler

What to Do

1. Hold the yardstick with one hand and place the tennis ball at the top edge of the yardstick.
2. Release the ball, and observe the height of the first bounce.
3. Repeat three times to get an average of the bouncing height.
4. Place the ball in a freezer for 30 minutes.
5. Again, measure the height that the ball bounces when released from the top of the yardstick.

174

FIG 2

6. Repeat three times and make note of any changes in the bounce height of each testing.

What Happened?

The ball does not bounce as high when it is cold. At a lower temperature, the gas molecules inside the ball move slower and have less kinetic energy. Thus, a ball filled with cold air will have a lower pressure than the same ball filled with hot air. A ball with low **air pressure** is essentially partially deflated and doesn't bounce very high. When testing the ball at room temperature, the bounce height should be relatively the same in each trial. When testing the freezer ball, the height of the bounce may increase with each trial because the ball is warming up to room temperature! Measuring with a yardstick makes it easy to observe the effect of temperature on the bounciness of a ball filled with air.

50. Coandă Effect

The Coandă effect is the tendency of a flowing fluid, either a liquid or a gas, to cling to a flat or convex surface in its path. Air flowing over a curved airplane wing clings to the wing just as flowing water will cling to a convex surface.

See for Yourself

Materials
pencil
large paper cup
bowl
tap water
plastic spoon
helper

What to Do
1. Push the pencil through the bottom of the cup.
2. With your finger over the hole, fill the cup with water.
3. Hold the cup about 1 foot (30 cm) above the top of the bowl.
4. Remove your finger from the hole and observe the direction the water flows out of the cup and into the bowl.
5. Ask your helper to repeat steps #2 and #3.
6. When your helper releases the water, hold the back of the spoon's bowl in the path of the falling water (Figure 1). Observe the path of the water.
7. While the water flows, slowly pull the spoon away from the water and this time observe the movement of the spoon instead of the water.

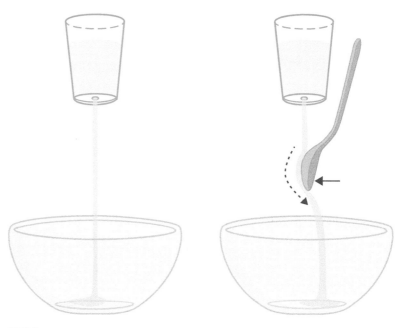

FIG 1

What Happened?

The water flows out of the hole in a vertical stream in response to the downward pull of gravity. When the outside, convex curve of the spoon's bowl is placed in the water's path, the water clings to the curved surface of the spoon and flows along the spoon. This is referred to as the Coandă effect. At the end of the spoon, the water continues to flow vertically in response to gravity, which pulls everything toward the center of Earth. When the spoon is pulled out of the water, there is a tendency for the flowing water to stay **attracted** to the convex surface of the spoon; thus, you feel a tug on the spoon when trying to remove it from the water.

178

51. Bernoulli's Principle

Bernoulli's principle states that an increase in the speed of **fluid** results in a decrease in pressure. This pressure does not refer to the pressure of a fast-moving fluid striking an object. Instead, it refers to the internal pressure of the fluid that pushes out in all directions. Basically, Bernoulli described the pressure that fast-moving fluids have on the surfaces over which they pass. Airplane wings are designed so that air flowing across the top of the wing moves faster than the air passing on the underside of the wing. Due to this design, the downward pressure of air on the wing's top surface is always less than the air pressure pushing up beneath the wing. This difference in air pressure provides a lift to the wings. In this activity watch for unequal fluid pressure, which can cause an object to move.

See for Yourself

Materials

2 books of equal size
sheet of notebook paper
drinking straw
ruler

What to Do

1. Position the books 4 inches (10 cm) apart on a table.
2. Use the paper as a bridge connecting the two books.
3. Place the end of the straw under the edge in the middle of the sheet of paper.

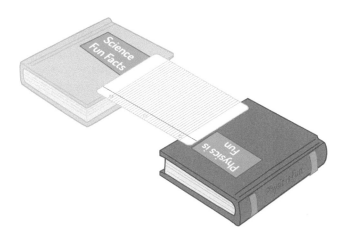

FIG 1

4. Blow as hard as you can through the straw under the paper.

FIG 2

180

What Happened?

The paper bridge bends downward toward the table when air is blown under it. Before blowing under the paper, air pressure on the paper was equal in all directions. According to the Bernoulli principle, increasing the speed of air causes a decrease in air pressure. It is observed that blowing a fast stream of air under the paper bridge decreased the air pressure. This resulted in a difference in pressure above and below the paper bridge. The higher air pressure above the bridge pushed the paper down. This is also commonly known as the Bernoulli Effect.

52. Pressure Differences

The shape of an airplane wing is designed so that air flows at different speeds across its top and bottom surfaces. A similar principle is happening with the sails on a boat. With a sail, the pressure on the inside is greater than on the outside of the sail; thus, the sail is pushed forward taking the boat with it. The speed of moving air, or any moving fluid, affects the pressure it applies to surfaces over which it moves. Bernoulli's principle states: The faster a fluid moves, the lower the pressure the fluid exerts on the surface over which it passes. Any time the speed of air is increased, it creates a low-pressure area. In Figure 1, the ping-pong ball cannot be blown out of the funnel because the air blown into the funnel stem creates a low-pressure area below the ball. The ambient air pressure keeps the ball in place. Surprisingly, you cannot blow a ping-pong ball out of a funnel.

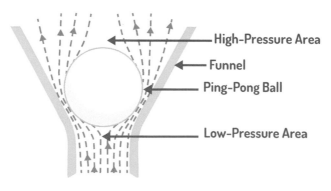

— High-Pressure Area

— Funnel

— Ping-Pong Ball

— Low-Pressure Area

FIG 1

182

See for Yourself

Materials

ping-pong ball
long-stemmed small funnel with smooth sides

What to Do

1. Place the ball inside the bowl of the upright funnel.
2. Try to blow the ball out of the funnel by blowing air through the stem of the funnel.

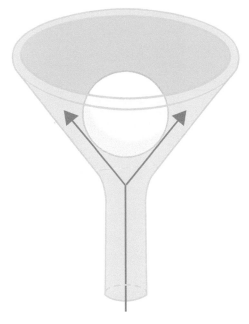

FIG 2

What Happened?

Before you blew into the funnel, the pressure of the air above, below, and around the ball was the same. Blowing a fast stream of air through the stem created a low-pressure area below the ball. The ambient air pressure surrounding the open end of the funnel was higher and this air pushed the ball downward. Blowing the ball out of the funnel is a task that sounds deceptively simple, but due to the laws of physics you cannot blow the ping-pong ball out of the funnel.

53. Balanced Forces

Balanced forces are forces of equal magnitude (size) acting in opposite directions on an object. Force is a push or pulling action that causes an object to move. When all the opposing forces on an object add up to zero, the forces are said to be balanced. **Levitation** is the action of rising and being held aloft, or up in the air, with only air providing the lift. **Lift** is an upward force on an object. In Figure 1, the air from a hairdryer provides the lift that levitates the ping-pong ball. Gravity is the opposing force. When these two opposing forces are equal, the ping-pong ball, seemingly by magic, remains suspended in the air.

See for Yourself

Materials

ping-pong ball

hairdryer

Even on low heat, the hairdryer can get hot, so do not keep the dryer on for an extended time and do not touch the open end.

What to Do

1. Turn on the hairdryer to its highest speed and coolest setting.
2. Point the hairdryer toward the ceiling.
3. Hold the ping-pong ball in the center of the airflow from the dryer, and then release the ball.
4. Slowly move the hairdryer back and forth (Figure 2). Observe the movement of the ping-pong ball.

185

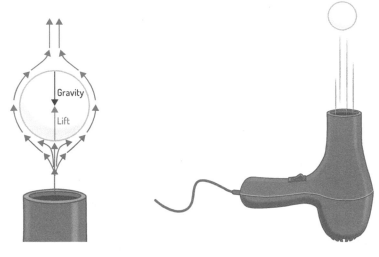

FIG 1   **FIG 2**

5. Slowly lean the end of the hairdryer a few degrees to the right and then to the left (Figure 3).

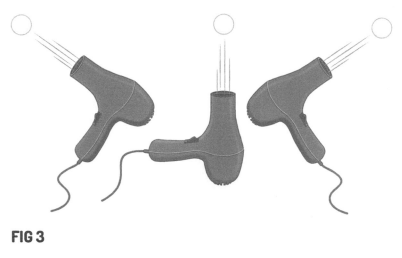

FIG 3

What Happened?

The suspended height of the levitating ball allows us to observe the results of two equal but opposite forces acting on an object. The two forces are said to be balanced. First, due to what is called the **Coandă effect**, the stream of air clings to and flows around the curved sides of the ball, and then continues moving forward. This creates the lift that overcomes the gravitational pull on the ping-pong ball. The ball floats in the center of the air stream and remains at the same distance from the end of the hairdryer.

Can the ping-pong ball escape the airstream? According to the **Bernoulli principle**, an increase in the **velocity** of a fluid decreases its pressure. If the ball gets too close to the edge of this column of upward-moving air, it is pushed back by the higher air pressure surrounding the air column. When the force of the air that is lifting the ball is equal to the force of the gravity pulling the ball down, the ball remains suspended at the same height above the hairdryer. What would happen if the uplifting force was increased? Discover for yourself in the following activity, #54 Unbalanced Forces.

54. Unbalanced Forces

Unbalanced forces are forces with different magnitudes acting in opposite directions on an object. In the previous activity, #53 "Balanced Forces," a ping-pong ball was held aloft, levitated, by an airstream produced by a hairdryer. As the ball was suspended above the end of the hairdryer, the height of the ball depended on the force of air beneath the ball. The ball was lifted until the force of the air pushing the ball upward equaled Earth's gravitational force pulling it down. The two forces were equal but in opposite directions; thus, they were balanced. If the lifting force is increased, the forces acting on the ball will be unbalanced. With a higher lifting force, the ball will rise higher above the hairdryer.

See for Yourself

Materials
ping-pong ball
hairdryer

Even on low heat, the hairdryer can get hot, so do not keep the dryer on for an extended time and do not touch the open end.

What to Do
1. Turn on the hairdryer to its highest speed and coolest heat setting.
2. Point the hairdryer toward the ceiling.
3. Hold the ping-pong ball in the airflow from the dryer, and then release the ball. Observe the height of the ping-pong ball above the nozzle of the hairdryer.

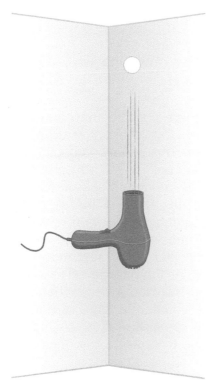

FIG 1

4. Move to the corner of a room with nothing hanging on the walls nearby. Repeat the previous steps holding the hairdryer near but not touching the walls.
5. Observe the height of the ping-pong ball above the end of the hairdryer.
6. Compare the height in step #3 with the height in step #5.

What Happened?

When the ball is levitated away from the wall, the air striking the bottom of the ball bounces off the ball and can move outward.

When the hairdryer is positioned close to the corner of the wall, the ping-pong ball levitates at a higher distance above the end of the hairdryer. This occurs because the air that strikes the bottom of the ball moves outward; this expanding air hits the wall and bounces back under the ball resulting in an increase in the force of the air lifting the ball. The upward force is greater than the downward force of gravity; thus, the two forces are unbalanced. When unbalanced forces act on an object, the object moves in the direction of the larger force. As the ball moves upward, the force of the air under the ball decreases. When the force of the air under the ball equals the force of Earth's gravity pulling it down, the ball remains aloft in this higher position. This activity allows us to observe the results of two unbalanced forces.

55. Lift Forces

Lift forces are upward acting forces on an object. A lift force can be produced by a fluid flowing around the object's surface. In Figure 1, the lift is the net upward force created by the air flow around the ball. As shown, there is a higher pressure under the ball than above it. This difference in pressure is due to the speed of the air flow around the ball. Because of the shape of the ball, the air flow below it is slower than the air flow above it (Figure 1). The **Bernoulli principle** states that as the speed of a fluid flowing over a surface increases, the pressure of that fluid on the surfaces decreases. Thus, due to the speed of air above and below the ball, there is a net upward force, which is lift, acting on it. Keep Bernoulli's principle in mind in the next activity as you blow into the bottom spout of the funnel. No matter your effort, the ball will refuse to come out of the funnel.

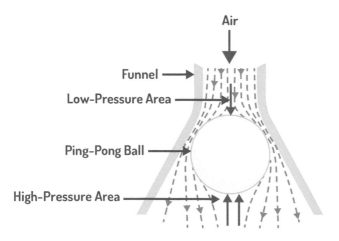

Air

Funnel →

Low-Pressure Area

Ping-Pong Ball →

High-Pressure Area

FIG 1

See for Yourself

Materials

long-stemmed small funnel with smooth sides
ping-pong ball

What to Do

1. Turn the funnel upside down.
2. Hold the ping-pong ball inside the funnel with your finger.
3. Start blowing into the narrow end of the funnel.
4. Remove your finger from the ball while continuing to blow into the funnel.

What Happened?

When you blow a stream of air downward, the ball will be suspended inside the funnel. As you are blowing downward, the air stream that is created is moving along the sides of the ball. The speed of the air blown into the funnel is faster than the speed of the air beneath the ball. Bernoulli compared the speed of a fluid to the pressure the fluid exerts on the surface it passes over. Thus, the faster the speed of the airstream as it passes around the ball, the less pressure it exerts upon the ball. The air pressure above the ball is greatly decreased compared with the pressure under the ball, so it remains suspended in the funnel. Like an airplane wing, the higher pressure beneath the ball provides lift that keeps the ball from falling. The lift is strong enough to overcome the downward pull of gravity on the ball.

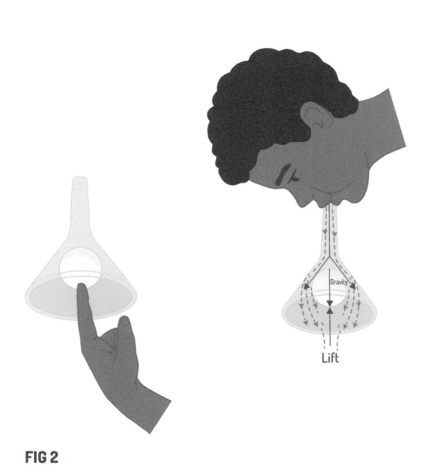

FIG 2

193

III
Simple Machines Introduction

Simple machines are devices that make work easier and have few moving parts. The scientific definition of **work** is the force applied to an object times the distance the object moves. The equation for work is:

$$W = F(\text{force}) \times d(\text{distance})$$

$$W = F \times d \quad or \quad W = Fd$$

The SI unit for work is the **joule**, which means that a force of one newton moved an object a distance of one meter. Another unit for work is foot-pound. One foot-pound is equal to 1.3558 joules.

Every job requires a specific amount of work. Ignoring friction, the output work of the machine would equal the input work that you put in. Output work is the product of the weight (load force) times the distance the load is moved. The input work is the effort force applied to the machine and the distance this force moves. The equation for this is:

$$\text{output work} = \text{input work}$$

or

$$F_{load} \times d_{load} = F_{effort} \times d_{effort}$$

Some machines can make a job easier by allowing you to apply less force, but others require you to apply more force than the load being lifted. The **mechanical advantage (MA)** is a measure of how a machine affects your effort force (see p197 for definitions of forces on levers). If the MA = 1, the effort and load forces are equal; thus, the machine doesn't make the work easier, but it does change the direction the effort force is applied to move a load force. If the MA > 1, the effort force is less than the load. If the MA < 1, the effort force is greater than the load force. The activities in this unit will identify the mechanical advantage of each simple machine that is investigated. You will discover the advantage of using machines that do not reduce the effort force needed. The two equations that can be used for calculating mechanical advantage are:

$$MA = \frac{\text{load force}}{\text{effort force}}$$

$$MA = \frac{\text{effort distance}}{\text{load distance}}$$

The six simple machines are:

1. lever,
2. inclined plane,
3. wedge,
4. screw,
5. wheel and axle, and
6. pulley.

196

Levers

A **lever** is any straight rigid object, such as a bar, resting on a pivot. The parts of a lever are: the lever, which is a simple rigid rod, and the **fulcrum**, which is any solid object that supports the lever. The lever can pivot around the fulcrum. A force applied to the lever is called the **effort force**; what is being moved is called the **load**, and the force it applies to the lever is called the **load force**. The distance between the effort force and the fulcrum is called the **effort distance** (also know as the **effort arm**). The distance between the load and the fulcrum is called the **load distance** (also know as the **load arm**).

There are three classes of lever that differ in the location of the fulcrum. The first- and second-class levers have a mechanical advantage, meaning they increase the effort force; on the other hand, the third-class lever reduces the effort force.

- A first-class lever has the fulcrum between the load and effort force. A seesaw is an example of a first-class lever.
- A second-class lever has the fulcrum at one end with the load between the fulcrum and the effort force. A wheelbarrow or a nut cracker is an example of a second-class lever.
- A third-class lever has the fulcrum at one end, and the effort force in between the fulcrum and the load. Tweezers are an example of a third-class lever.

Inclined Plane

An **inclined plane** is a flat surface that is raised at one end. This machine makes moving heavy objects to a higher surface easier than lifting the object vertically.

Wedge

A **wedge** is a device that forces things apart. A wedge has a shape as if two inclined planes were put together back to back.

Screw

A **screw** is a special type of inclined plane that is used to lift things, such as a screw jack, or to hold things together.

Pulley

A **pulley** changes the direction of the input force. A pulley uses a wheel with a groove and a rope. One end of the rope is attached to the load, and the other end is where the input force or effort force is applied. Pulleys do not always multiply the effort force; instead, pulleys change the direction of the input force. Lifting a load vertically is harder than lifting the load using a pulley and pulling down on the rope.

Wheel and Axle

A **wheel and axle** is a wheel with a rod attached in the middle. This machine, in some cases, is like a lever that multiplies the effort force, such as a doorknob. In many cases, a wheel and axle make it easier to move an object, such as a wagon full of bricks.

56. First-Class Lever

A **lever** is a rigid bar that rotates around a fixed point called a **fulcrum** or pivot point. A **first-class lever** has the fulcrum between the **load force** being lifted and the **effort force** needed to move the load. Figure 1 is a first-class lever with the fulcrum located in the center.

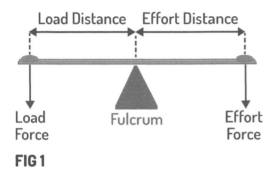

Load Distance   Effort Distance

Load Force   Fulcrum   Effort Force

FIG 1

Figure 2 is also a first-class lever with the fulcrum closer to the load. Like a seesaw, the ends of the lever arm rotate around the fulcrum. The levers in both Figures 1 and 2 are

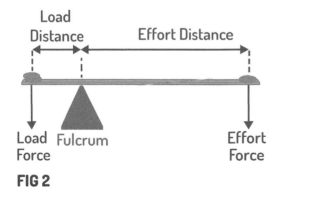

Load Distance   Effort Distance

Load Force   Fulcrum   Effort Force

FIG 2

199

horizontal, meaning they are balanced. This happens when the torque or turning forces on each side of the fulcrum are equal. Thus, the lever does not rotate.

Mechanical advantage is a measure of how much a **machine** helps you. The equation for measuring mechanical advantage is:

$$MA = \text{load force} / \text{effort force}$$

or

$$MA = \text{effort distance} / \text{load distance}$$

In Figure 1, the effort force and load force are equal, thus the MA = 1. With the fulcrum in this position, this machine only changes the direction the effort force has to be applied. If you want the load to be lifted, then the direction of the effort force is down.

In Figure 2, the effort force is less than the load force, thus the MA > 1. By placing the fulcrum closer to the load, the mechanical advantage of a first-class lever is increased. This means less effort force is needed.

See for Yourself

Materials
tape
round pencil
coins, pennies, or small metal washers of equal sizes and weights
wooden or nonflexible ruler

What to Do

1. Tape the pencil to a flat surface, such as a table. The pencil will act as the fulcrum.
2. Place one coin on each end of the ruler. The coins represent a load force and an effort force on the lever bar, which is the ruler.
3. Balance the lever bar (ruler) on the fulcrum (pencil). The lever bar will balance when the torque created by each coin is equal. Make note of where the fulcrum is under the lever bar.

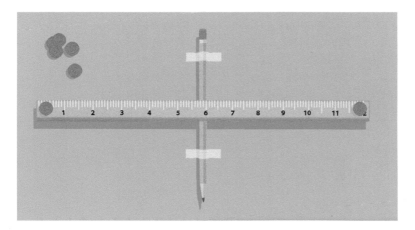

FIG 3

4. Increase the load force on one end by using four stacked coins and keep the one coin on the opposite end as the effort force. Repeat step #3.

What Happened?

The ruler and pencil form a first-class lever, which means the fulcrum is between the load and the effort force. In this activity, when the load and effort force were equal, the fulcrum was found to be in the center of the ruler; thus, the distance from each force to the fulcrum is the same.

When the force and distance for both the effort and load forces are the same, then the torque acting on each end of the ruler is equal; thus, there is no rotation and the ruler balances. Remember, when a first-class lever is balanced, the torque, turning force, on either side of the fulcrum is equal.

A first-class lever, can be used to multiply the effort force. In other words, a large load force can be lifted by a small effort force if the fulcrum is placed closer to the load. This makes the effort distance longer. So, using MA = effort distance/load distance, the MA > 1. This means the machine multiplies the effort force. This was observed when one coin (effort force) was able to support four coins (load force) because the fulcrum was closer to the load force.

57. Equal-Arm Balance

An **equal-arm balance** is an example of a first-class lever. It has the basic design of a seesaw with a beam that balances when the mass on either side of a pivot point is equal. A teeter totter at the park has a seat for each child on opposite ends. Likewise, an equal-arm balance also has a place where objects being compared are placed. In this activity, a simple equal-arm balance will be constructed and used to determine the unknown mass of an object.

See for Yourself

Materials

straw, straight
scissors
paper punch
2 index cards 3 × 5 inches (7.5 × 12.5 cm)
ruler
marking pen
2 wooden blocks of equal height or stacks of books
long needle
tape
adult helper

What to Do

1. Cut a 1 inch (2.5 cm) slit in each end of the straw. The slits should be at the same relative position on each end.
2. Fold both index cards in half by placing the short sides together. Cut along the fold.

3. Insert one paper piece in each slit on the ends of the straw. These papers will act as massing pans.

4. Use the ruler to find the center of the straw, mark this spot. With adult supervision, push the straight needle through the center of the straw, leaving an equal amount of the needle sticking out on each side of the straw. Move the needle around to hollow out the hole through the straw. You want the straw to freely rotate around it.

5. Position the two blocks on a table and place the ends of the needle on the top of each block. Secure the ends of the needle to the blocks with tape.

6. Move the paper massing pans in and out of the slits until the straw is horizontal, which means it is balanced.

7. Cut paper punches from one of the remaining paper halves. Draw a figure on the remaining paper half and cut it out.

8. Place the cut-out figure on one of the massing pans. Observe how the straw balance tips down on the side with the figure.

9. Add paper punches evenly distributed to the opposite massing pan until the straw-balance is again horizontal.

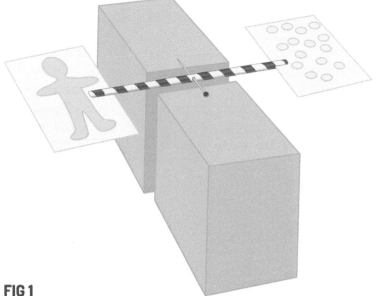

FIG 1

What Happened?

An equal-arm balance was made. When using an equal-arm balance to find the mass of an object, you place the object to be massed in one of the **massing pans**. Then you slowly add known masses to the massing pan on the opposite side until the pans balance. In this activity, each paper punch is given a mass of 1, thus the mass of the paper character is equivalent to the total number of paper punches needed to balance the paper character. Equal-arm balances are designed so that the distance from the pivot point is the same for both measuring pans. Thus, when the mass on each of the massing pans is equal, the torque or turning force is equal, and the straw will be horizontal.

58. Second-Class Lever

A **second-class lever** has the load between the fulcrum and the effort force as shown in Figure 1. Similar to a first-class lever, second-class levers are machines that can multiply your effort force. Changing the position of the load can affect the mechanical advantage of a second-class lever. Note the distance of the effort force to the fulcrum is not affected by the position of the load.

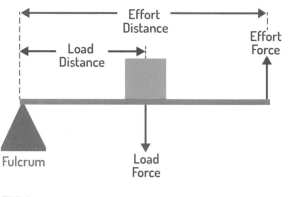

FIG 1

The mechanical advantage of this lever is equal to the ratio of the effort distance/load distance. This can be expressed by this equation:

$$MA = \frac{\text{effort distance}}{\text{load distance}}$$

206

The closer the load force is to the fulcrum, the shorter is the load distance, thus the MA > 1. Thus, as the load distance decreases the less effort force is needed.

See for Yourself

Materials

rocks 1 to 2 pounds (4.5 to 9 N) or any object to add weight
small bucket
duct tape
yardstick (meter stick)
spring scale (newtons, grams)
helper

What to Do

1. Place the rocks in the bucket.
2. Tape one end of the yardstick (meter stick) to the edge of a table.
3. Ask your helper to hang the bucket on the yardstick (meter stick) so that it is next to the table. With the bucket in this position, attach the spring scale to the free end of the yardstick. Read the unit measurement on the scale in newtons (Figure 2).
4. While holding the yardstick in a horizontal position, ask your helper to move the bucket to the center of the yardstick. Read the unit measurement on the scale in newtons.
5. While holding the yardstick in a horizontal position, ask your helper to move the bucket to the end of the yardstick. Read the unit measurement on the scale in newtons.

FIG 2

What Happened?

The effort distance doesn't change in a second-class lever no matter where the load is. The position of the load is what affects the mechanical advantage of a second-class lever.

The closer the load is to the fulcrum, the shorter the load distance and the greater is the mechanical advantage. In this activity, you discovered that the closer the load force is to the fulcrum, the less effort force it took to lift the bucket. The fulcrum and the effort distance remain stationary in a second-class lever. Thus, it is the position of the load force that determines the mechanical advantage. As the load distance decreases, the effort force also decreases.

59. Third-Class Lever

A **third-class lever** has the effort between the fulcrum and the load. In Figure 1, the load distance remains constant while the effort distance changes. There is no mechanical advantage for using this type of lever, which means the machine doesn't reduce the effort force needed to move a load force. In other words, when using a third-class lever, it takes more effort to move a load. When using this type of lever, the load is always moved a greater distance and at a faster speed than is the effort force. Remember that effort is a force exerted by you on simple machines. A broom is an example of a third-class lever. In Figure 1, the fulcrum of the broom is at one end. You apply an effort force between the fulcrum and the load to be moved. Your effort force moves a smaller distance and the load moves a greater distance. Thus, when sweeping, you move the debris a greater distance.

See for Yourself

Materials
2 yardsticks (meter sticks)
tape
empty box (measuring about 4 inches (10 cm) on each side)

What to Do
1. Hold the two yardsticks (meter sticks) together and tape two of the ends together.

Third-Class Lever

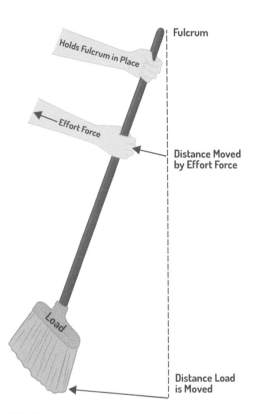

Fulcrum

Holds Fulcrum in Place

Effort Force

Distance Moved
by Effort Force

Load

Distance Load
is Moved

FIG 1

2. Hold the sticks, one in each hand about 6 inches (15 cm) from the free ends.
3. Press the ends of the sticks against the box, one on each side of the box.
4. Try to lift the box and move it about 12 inches (30 cm) (Figure 2).

211

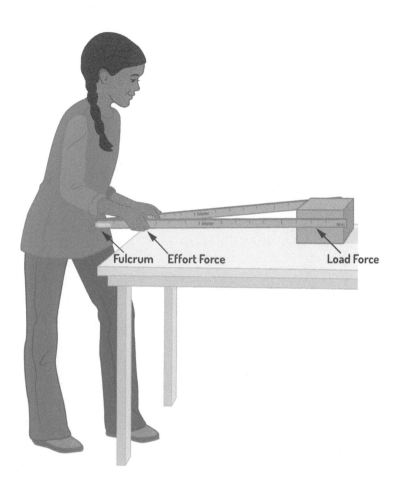

Fulcrum   Effort Force   Load Force

FIG 2

5. Grasp the box with your fingers and move it back to the original position.

212

What Happened?

Taping the sticks together forms a device similar to a pair of tongs, which is an example of a double third-class lever. The taped ends form the fulcrum. Your hands are applying a force between the fulcrum and the load being lifted. It required more effort to lift the box with the sticks than when lifting the box directly with your fingers. This is because a third-class lever reduces your effort force. Are you wondering if third-class levers are useful machines? Actually, they are very helpful when handling delicate objects, because they reduce the force you apply, for example when using tweezers. If you want to move the load a distance, a broom or a rake might be the third-class lever for the job. And don't forget the helpful tongs that you use to choose your salad toppings!

60. Just for Fun: Third-Class Lever

A third-class lever has the effort force between the load and fulcrum. This type of lever does not magnify the effort force as do the first- and second-class levers. Instead, the third-class lever reduces the effort force and increases the distance the load is moved. In other words, the effort force moves a small distance while the load moves a larger distance. A fishing pole is an example of a third-class lever.

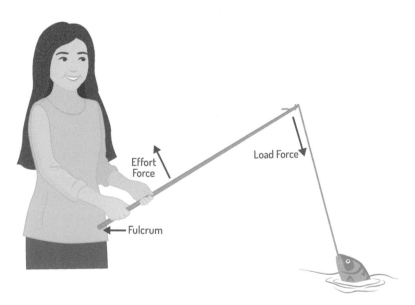

FIG 1

See for Yourself

Materials

1 yard (1 m) piece of string

yardstick (meter stick)

metal screw ring for canning jars (any 2½ inch (6.4 cm) metal ring)

1 L empty plastic soda bottle and lid

tap water

What to Do

1. Tie one end of the string to the end of the yardstick (meter stick) and tie the other end of the string to the metal ring.
2. Fill the plastic soda bottle with water and close it with its lid.
3. Set the bottle on the floor.
4. Hold the free end of the yardstick (meter stick) as you would hold a fishing pole, one hand above the other. Use the top hand to raise and lower the yardstick, thus raising and lowering the dangling metal ring. The top hand will be called your effort hand.
5. Stand so that the metal ring dangles above the top of the bottle and try to place the ring over the bottle by moving the end of the yardstick (Figure 2).
6. Raise and lower the dangling ring using only your effort hand to change the position of the yardstick.

FIG 2

What Happened?

Most find this task difficult because small movements of your effort hand result in large movements of the load. This makes it difficult to place the ring in a specific spot. Does this lever experience help you to understand why some carnival games are hard to win? Yes, the game that looks so simple involves the use of levers!

61. Inclined Plane

An inclined plane is a slanting or sloping surface used to raise an object to a higher level. The mechanical advantage of an inclined plane is determined by dividing the length of the sloping surface by the height of the raised end. The mechanical advantage is always greater than one for inclined planes because it takes less effort to move a load up an inclined plane than it would to lift the load vertically. Ignoring friction between the load and the sloped surface, the amount of work needed to lift the load vertically to a specific height is equal to the amount of work needed to push or pull the load up an inclined plane to that same height.

See for Yourself

Materials
scissors
wide rubber band
ruler
3 or more books
yardstick (meter stick)
cup of rice
sock
string, 18 inches (45 cm)

What to Do
1. Stack the books on a table and place one end of the yardstick (meter stick) on the books to form a ramp (inclined plane).

2. Cut the rubber band to make one long strip. Lay the rubber strip on the ruler, pulling one end of the rubber strip over the top of the ruler and taping it to the back of the ruler.

3. Pour the rice into the sock, and tie one end of the string around the top of the sock to secure the rice and the other end to the free end of the rubber strip.

4. Move the load by raising it straight up: Place the sock on the table next to the stacked books, and then lift the ruler-scale straight up until the sock is at a height equal to that of the stacked books.

5. Observe the distance the rubber band stretches along the ruler.

6. Move the load by pulling it up the ramp: Place the sock on the bottom of the ramp, and holding the scale slowly pull the sock to the top of the ramp (Figure 1).

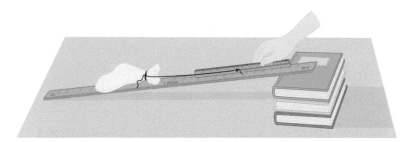

FIG 1

7. Again, observe the distance the rubber band stretches as the sock is being pulled up the ramp.

218

What Happened?

The rubber band stretched less when you pulled the sock up the ramp than when you lifted it straight up. This means it took less force to drag the load up the ramp than to lift it straight up. The same amount of work was done with each method, but your effort force is reduced when using an inclined plane. Thus, the mechanical advantage of an inclined plane is greater than one. It is interesting to note that when using an inclined plane, you have to move the load a greater distance, but it takes less force to do so. Therefore, we can say it was easier. Next time you see a moving truck in the street, you might notice the movers taking advantage of an inclined plane!

62. Screw

A **screw** is an inclined plane that is wrapped around a cylinder to form spiraling ridges. Screws look like small, spiral staircases. A common example of a screw is a wood screw, which has a sharp point that acts like a wedge. The point enters the wood creating a path for its spiraling inclined plane to cut its way in.

Wood screws are generally right-handed, meaning that when looking from the pointed end of the screw, the ridges spiral in a clockwise direction, and when rotated, the ridges appear to be moving toward you.

See for Yourself

Materials

ruler

pencil

plane paper, white

black marker

tape

What to Do

1. Draw a right triangle on the sheet of paper with a base of 4 inches (10 cm) and a height of 6 inches (15 cm).
2. Cut out the triangle.
3. Color the diagonal edge of the triangle with the black marker.
4. Tape the triangle to the pencil, with the colored edge facing up. It is important that the triangle is attached as shown in Figure 1.

220

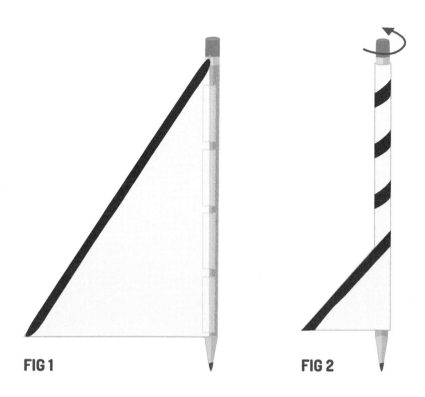

FIG 1　　　　　　**FIG 2**

5. Rotate the pencil counterclockwise so the paper winds around the pencil; secure the end of the paper triangle with tape (Figure 2).
6. Count the number of diagonal stripes made by the colored edge of the triangle that is wrapped around the pencil.
7. Hold the pencil horizontally with the point facing you as in Figure 3. In this position, observe the stripes as you turn the pencil clockwise.

FIG 3

What Happened?

Each colored band on the paper around the pencil represents a **spiral ridge** on a screw, which is called a thread. The **pitch** of a screw is determined by the number of threads in 1 inch (2.5 cm). The smaller the pitch the greater the mechanical advantage, meaning it is easier to turn the screw. The model in this activity represents a wood screw, which is a **right-handed screw**; thus, the threads slant to the right and when rotated clockwise the threads appear to move toward the pointed end. A right-handed wood screw is designed to turn clockwise as it moves forward boring into the wood. Keeping in mind this information about a wood screw, you will easily be able to remember the rhyme that teaches the direction to turn the screwdriver for a screw to tighten or loosen: "Righty Tighty, Lefty Loosey."

63. Wedge

A **wedge** is a simple machine shaped like an inclined plane. You can think of a wedge as a moveable inclined plane. Instead of an object being pushed or pulled up a slanted surface, the slanted surface (the wedge) moves forward and raises the object. In a manner similar to an inclined plane, the longer the raised surface of the wedge, the greater the mechanical advantage (MA) of this machine. The effort force always pushes the wedge forward causing the load, the object being moved, to move to the side that is perpendicular to the direction of the effort force. For example, if a wedge is moved under an object, the object moves up. The **slope** of a wedge is a measure of how steep the slanted edge is. The more gradual a slope, the longer will be the effort distance, thus the less effort is needed to lift the load.

See for Yourself

Materials
pencil
ruler
thick cardboard
marker
scissors
small paperback book

What to Do
1. Draw two right triangles on the cardboard, one with a base of 6 inches (15 cm) and a height of 5 inches (12.5 cm); the second with a base of 10 inches (25 cm) and a height of 5 inches (12.5 cm).

2. With the marker, draw a line across the base of each triangle. On this line, print the length of each base.

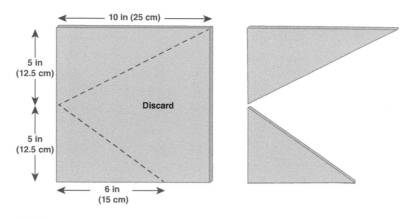

FIG 1

3. Cut out the two triangles from the cardboard piece.
4. Lay the book on a table.
5. Hold the small cardboard triangle upright with its 6 inch (15 cm) base against the table.
6. Support the book as shown in Figure 2 so that it does not move forward as you gently push the wedge under the book.

224

FIG 2

7. Make note of the direction the book moves and the height the book can be raised with the wedge.

8. Repeat steps #4 through #7 using the larger wedge.

What Happened?

As the cardboard wedges are pushed forward, the book is raised. The wedges are of equal height, but one has a smaller base. The wedge with the longer base has a more gradual slope and should have been easier to slide under the book. The tapered edges of the two wedges first slid under the book allowing the gradual widening of the wedge to follow. A wedge acts like an inclined plane, except it is the wedge that moves under the load instead of the load being pulled up the incline.

225

64. Moveable Pulley

A pulley is a machine that consists of a wheel, usually grooved, that holds a cord. A **moveable pulley** is able to move with the load that is being moved. Moveable pulleys allow you to use less force to raise an object than if you lifted it vertically without the pulley. The mechanical advantage of moveable pulleys is equal to the number of supporting cords. For a single moveable pulley, the MA = 2, which means by using the moveable pulley it takes half as much effort force to lift a load.

See for Yourself

Materials
string, 12 inches (30 cm)
empty thread or ribbon spool
metal paper clip
ribbon, 36 inches (90 cm) and about half the width of the groove in the thread spool
tape
toy bucket of rocks used in Activity #58 Second-Class Lever
spring scale
helper

What to Do
1. Thread the string through the hole in the thread spool, and tie the ends of the string together.
2. Attach the paper clip to the string, and open one side of the clip to form a hook.

226

3. Secure one end of the ribbon to the edge of a table using the tape.

4. Run the ribbon around the grooves of the thread spool, and then attach the spring scale to the free end of the ribbon.

5. While holding the spring scale, ask a helper to attach the bucket to the paper clip hook. Pull up on the spring scale to raise the bucket by about 1 foot (30 cm), and then read the scale measurement.

FIG 1

227

6. Remove the bucket and place it on the floor. Next, use the spring scale to measure the force needed to lift the bucket about 1 foot (30 cm) upward from the floor.

What Happened?

The spool acts as a moveable pulley, which moves in the same direction as the load that is being raised. The moveable pulley in this activity has two supporting cords; therefore, the mechanical advantage of the pulley is 2. This means that when using this pulley, your effort is multiplied by 2.

65. Fixed Pulley

A **fixed pulley** stays in place; the pulley turns as the cord moves over the wheel, and a load is raised as the cord is pulled down. A fixed pulley makes work easier, not by reducing the effort force needed, but by changing the direction of the effort force. This type of pulley has one supporting cord, which is the cord tied to the load force. The mechanical advantage of a pulley is equal to its number of supporting cords. For a single fixed pulley, MA = 1. While this pulley doesn't multiply your effort force, it is easier to pull down on the cord to raise the load than to pull up on the load itself. With a mechanical advantage of one, the effort force and load are equal as well as the effort distance and load distance.

See for Yourself

Materials
empty thread spool
pencil (skinny enough to slide through the hole in the spool)
string, 6 feet (1.8 m)
ruler
clothespin
marker
helper

What to Do
1. Push the pencil through the hole in the thread spool. The spool must turn easily on the pencil.

2. Make a loop out of the string by tying both ends together. Then, place the string loop over the thread spool.

3. Lay the spool with the pencil and string on a table. Move the string so that the knot is positioned in the middle, and then directly across from the knot, mark the middle of the string on the other side of the loop as shown in Figure 1.

4. Ask a helper to hold the ends of the pencil at arm's length over their head. Make sure the string does not touch anything.

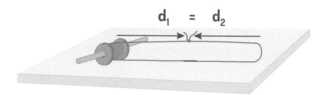

$$d_1 = d_2$$

FIG 1

5. Attach one clothespin to the knot in the middle of the string coming from behind the spool. The clothespin represents the load force.

6. Holding the string where it is marked, pull down on the string until the clothespin is raised to the top. Note how far you pulled the mark on the string down, and compare the distance that the clothespin was raised.

230

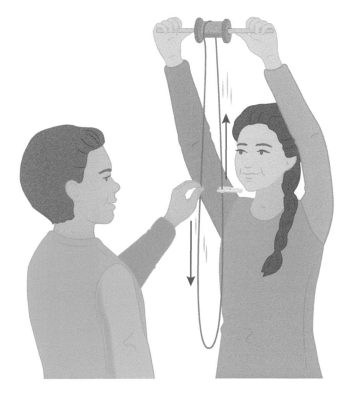

FIG 2

What Happened?

The thread spool acts as a single fixed pulley; thus, it has a MA = 1. This means that it takes the same effort to lift the load by pulling down on the string as it would to lift it straight up without the pulley. The input work done on the machine is equal to the effort force times the distance the effort force moved. Ignoring friction, the input work is equal to the output work, which is the work done on the load. The equation expressing this relationship is:

$$F_{effort} \times d_{effort} = F_{load} \times d_{load}$$

Look carefully at the equation and you will notice that if the effort force is equal to the load force, then, for this equation to balance, the effort distance must equal the load distance. You found this to be true for the single fixed pulley in this activity. Neglecting any loss by friction, you will find this to be true for all simple machines that have a MA = 1.

This activity modeled the single fixed pulley used at the top of a flag pole. Even though it doesn't affect your effort force, it would be easiest to raise a flag by pulling down on a cord.

66. Wheel and Axle

A **wheel and axle** is a simple machine made up of an axle attached to a wheel. The mechanical advantage of this machine is equal to the diameter of the wheel divided by the diameter of the axle. Since the wheel is always larger than the axle, the mechanical advantage is always greater than one; thus, the effort force is always less than the load force.

See for Yourself

Materials
empty thread spool
2 pencils
2 pieces of string, 24 inches (60 cm)
tape
2 pieces of string, 36 inches (90 cm)
metal paper clips

What to Do
1. Stick the pointed end of one pencil through the center of the empty thread spool. Repeat with the other pencil, sticking it into the other end of the spool. Be sure that the pencils fit snugly and do not slide. If the pencils are loose, wrap a piece of paper around the end before sticking it into the spool.

   You have made a wheel and axle.

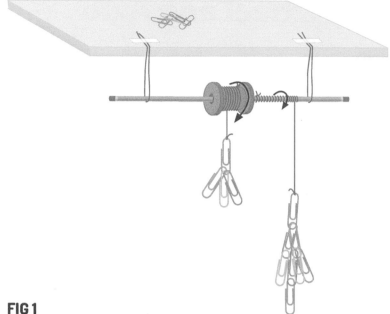

FIG 1

2. Use the two shorter strings to form loops to suspend the wheel and axle as shown in Figure 1. Use tape to secure the string to the top edge of a table. Make sure the wheel and axle hang level.

3. Tie one paper clip on the end of each of the two remaining strings. Bend the ends of the paper clips outward to form a hook.

4. Tape the free end of one of the strings to the center of the thread spool. Rotate the pencils away from you so that the string wraps over the top of the spool. Tape the paper clip to the spool so the string will not unwind.

234

5. Tape the remaining string to the pencil. Turn the pencils toward you so the string is wound in the opposite direction than the string on the spool.
6. Add eight paper clips to the hook on the string around the pencil. The string should be long enough for the paper clip load to rest on the floor.
7. Remove the paper clip hook taped to the spool and allow it to hang freely. Add paper clips to this hook until the load begins to rise. Determine the number of paper clips needed to raise the load up to the pencil. Observe the distance that each string moves.

What Happened?

The thread spool acts as a wheel while the pencils form the axle. The diameter of the spool is greater than the diameter of the pencils. Thus, with each rotation, more string moves down from the spool than from the pencil. The weight attached to the spool's string moves farther, but it takes less weight to raise the heavier load attached to the pencil axle. The spool and pencil form a machine called a wheel and axle.

IV
Magnets Introduction

Magnetism is the **magnetic force** of attraction or repulsion between magnets and **magnetic materials**. In this introduction to magnetism, several activities will show why some materials are attracted to a magnet while others are not. In another activity, an invisible magnetic field is made visible by mapping it.

Coercivity may be an unfamiliar term, but it is simply a measure of how resistant a magnetic material is to changes in magnetization. Some magnets have a high coercivity; thus; they are less affected by factors that reduce magnetic strength. These are called **permanent magnets**. **Temporary magnets** have a low coercivity. They must remain in the magnetic field of another magnet to retain their magnetism. Several activities will compare these types of magnet.

Electromagnetic contains a word part that sounds like electricity and helps you to remember that, in these magnets, electricity plays a key role. When an electric current is flowing through a conductive wire, a magnetic field forms around the wire. This magnetic field is generally weak. The magnetic field can be made stronger by wrapping the wire into a coil that is called a **solenoid**. Increasing the number of coils in the wire and placing a magnetic material in the center of the coil also increases the magnetic strength of an **electromagnet**. An electromagnet only works when a current is flowing. Turn off the electric current and the magnetic field produced by the current is gone. But, the magnetic core of the solenoid generally is a material with low coercivity, meaning it is only temporarily magnetized. Soft iron is one metal used for the core of a solenoid, because of its low coercivity. You will experience creating an electromagnet by making a solenoid of insulated wire with an iron nail as the core. Beyond just making an electromagnet, you will test its magnetic properties and discover how to use your right hand as a testing device to determine the polarity of your electromagnet. Magnetic polarity is the direction of a magnet's north and south poles.

Cardinal directions are north, south, east, and west, and their symbols are, respectively, N, S, E, and W. A **compass rose** is a diagram showing these directions and it is found on a compass as well as on maps. But there is a difference between compass and map directions. The compass, containing a magnetic needle, lines up with Earth's magnetic field. Yes, there is a magnetic field surrounding Earth. No, there is not a ginormous magnet inside the Earth. The truth is that Earth's magnetic field is produced by an electromagnet. Remember, an electromagnet is produced by moving electrons (electricity). The outer core, deep inside the Earth is made of molten iron, which moves in the direction of Earth's rotation about its axis. This movement results in the movement of the free electrons in the molten iron. Since the Earth wobbles a bit as it moves through space during its yearly trip around the Sun, over time, the polarity of Earth's magnetic field changes. Thus, over long periods of time the location of Earth's Magnetic North Pole changes. Before heading out for Santa's North Pole, it is important to know the difference in True North, due North,

Magnetic North, and Geographic North. The activities in this unit will compare these different ways of expressing cardinal directions.

Magnetic permeability, the property of a material that does not allow magnetic lines of force to pass through, will be investigated. This material acts as a magnetic shield, which basically absorbs a magnetic field, thus protecting nearby materials that might be damaged by a magnetic field.

67. Ferromagnetism

Magnetism is the **magnetic force** of attraction or repulsion between magnets, or between magnets and ferromagnetic materials. **Ferromagnetism** is the unique ability of some materials, including iron, to exhibit magnetism. "Ferro" is a chemical term derived from the Latin word "*ferrum*" meaning iron. Iron is the most common magnetic material, thus the name ferromagnetism. Some materials like cobalt and nickel are called ferromagnetic, even though they don't contain iron, because they exhibit the property of magnetism.

Ferromagnetic materials are generally called **magnetic materials**. The difference between magnetic and non-magnetic materials is that magnetic materials have domains. A **magnetic domain** is a region in which the magnetic properties of atoms are aligned. These clusters of atoms behave like tiny magnets with their **magnetic poles** pointing in the same direction. Magnetic materials exhibit magnetism when their domains align. Otherwise, they have no magnetism. As you will discover, it is easy to magnetize magnetic materials, such as paper clips, by placing them on a magnet. This results in most or even all the magnetic domains lining up with each other (Figure 1). Rubbing a ferromagnetic material in one direction with a magnet is another way of reorganizing domains.

See for Yourself

Materials
magnet, the stronger the better
10 or more metal paper clips

Magnetic Domains

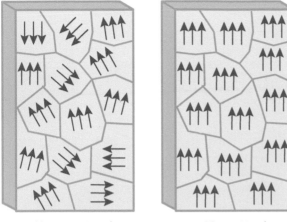

Unmagnetized   Magnetized

FIG 1

What to Do

1. Keep the magnet away from the paper clips so that it doesn't magnetize all the clips.
2. Hold the magnet in one hand and touch one paper clip to the end of the magnet.
3. Touch the end of a second paper clip to the end of the paper clip that is suspended from the magnet.
4. Repeat step #3 using the remaining paper clips. Place each new additional paper clip on the end of the chain as shown in Figure 2.

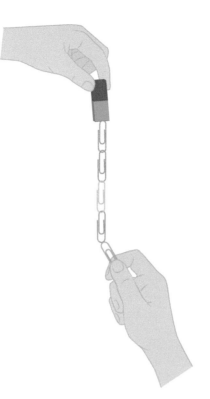

FIG 2

What Happened?

The paper clips, which are made of steel containing iron, have magnetic domains. Normally, the domains of ferro-magnetic materials are in random order, but when near or touching a magnet, the domains line up. It is observed that, in this case, a paper clip becomes temporarily magnetized. Understanding how to magnetize ferromagnetic objects greatly helps in the understanding of why magnets can become demagnetized when dropped. The impact of being dropped causes the domains to be jiggled out of order, which demagnetizes them.

68. Magnetic Field

All magnets are surrounded by an area called a **magnetic field**. This area is made of invisible magnetic field lines that point away from the north pole toward the south pole. Figure 1 shows magnetic field lines around a bar magnet.

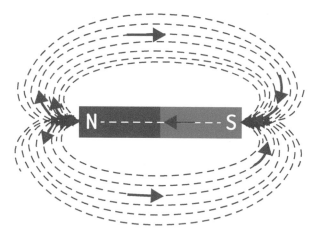

FIG 1

The magnetic field lines are closest together at the north (N) and south (S) poles, indicating that the poles have the strongest magnetic attraction.

244

See for Yourself

Materials

small metal paper clips, 1 box of 100
large bowl
2 strings, each 1 foot (30 cm)
bar magnet
pencil

What to Do

1. Spread the paper clips over the bottom of the bowl.
2. Tie one end of each string to each end of the bar magnet.
3. Tie the free ends of each string to a pencil.
4. Lift the magnet by pulling up on the pencil. The magnet should hang horizontally. An adjustment to the length of the strings may be needed.
5. Hold the magnet over the bowl and lower the magnet into the bowl until the magnet touches the paper clips.
6. Slowly raise the magnet and observe which part of the magnet attracted the most paper clips (Figure 3).

What Happened?

Metal paper clips are made of stainless steel, which contain iron. Thus, the paper clips contain a ferromagnetic material that is attracted to magnets. As shown in Figure 3,

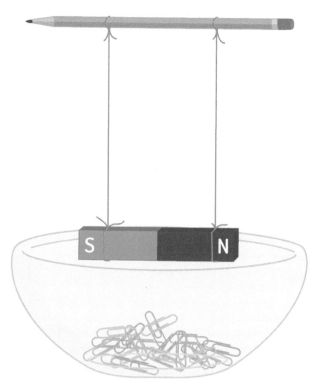

FIG 2

the magnetic field around a bar magnet is strongest at the north and south poles. More paper clips are attracted to the ends of the bar magnet, confirming that the poles of a bar magnet have the strongest magnetic fields.

246

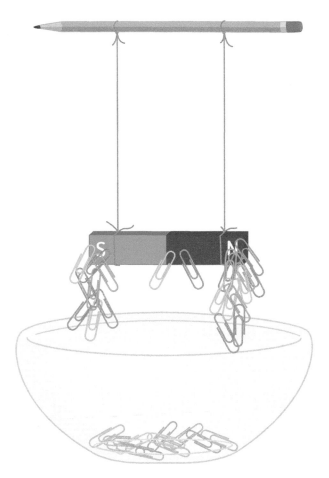

FIG 3

247

69. 3-D Magnetic Field

A magnetic field is an area around a magnet that exerts a magnetic force. By convention, the direction of a magnetic field points away from the north pole of a magnet toward the magnet's south pole. The shape of a magnetic field depends on the shape of the magnet, but all magnetic fields are three dimensional. Three dimensional (3-D) means the field envelops the magnet. Figure 1A shows magnetic field lines encircling a bar-shaped magnet. Figure 1B represents the direction of the field lines outside and inside the magnet. Inside the magnet, magnetic field lines move from the south pole to the north pole. Outside the magnet, the field lines encircle the magnet and move from the north pole to the south pole. Short slender pieces of magnetic materials placed on a magnet will demonstrate the three-dimensional shape of the magnetic field lines around a magnet.

A

B

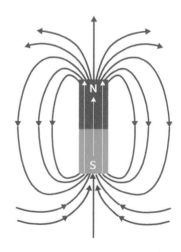

FIG 1

See for Yourself

Materials

magnets of different shapes: donut shaped, bar, U-shaped

white copy paper

scissors

pipe cleaner, 12 inches (30 cm)

What to Do

1. Lay the paper on a table, and place a magnet flat on the paper.
2. Cut the pipe cleaner into ½ inch (1.25 cm) pieces.
3. One by one touch the pipe cleaner pieces to different parts of the magnet. Observe the direction of each pipe cleaner.

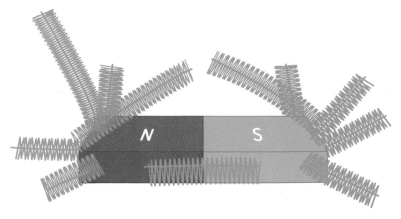

FIG 2

4. Repeat steps #1 through #3 using other different-shaped magnets.

What Happened?

The pipe cleaner pieces demonstrate the direction of magnetic field lines around a magnet. The pipe cleaner pieces make visible the otherwise invisible lines of a magnetic field. A magnetic field is an area around a magnet in which the force of the magnet affects the movement of magnetic objects. The bendable middle of a pipe cleaner is made of steel that contains iron. When the pipe cleaner pieces enter the magnetic field, the iron is attracted to the magnet. The pipe cleaners should make visible the direction of the three-dimensional magnetic field around magnets with different shapes.

70. Mapping Magnetic Fields

Magnetic fields are areas around an object that exhibit a magnetic influence. A magnetic object placed in a magnetic field is affected by this field. This effect will happen along the field lines. **Magnetic poles** are the points where the magnetic field lines begin and end. Field lines converge, or come together, at the poles. The direction of magnetic field lines is from the north pole of a magnet to the south pole. Although a magnetic field is invisible, we can prove it is there by watching the movement of objects affected while inside this field. In this activity, a compass will be placed inside a magnetic field. The movement of the magnetic needle inside of a compass will be used to map the direction of a magnetic field around a magnet.

See for Yourself

Materials
bar magnet
sheet of plain paper
small, round compass
pencil

What to Do
1. Place the magnet horizontally near the bottom edge of the sheet of paper.
2. Place the compass on the paper, about 1 inch (2.5 cm) above the north pole side of the magnet.

251

3. Use the pencil to mark a dot on the paper in front of the north pole of the compass pointer.
4. Move the compass forward a distance equal to the diameter of the compass and in the direction of the north pole of the compass needle.
5. Mark a new dot on the paper in front of the north pole of the compass pointer.
6. Repeat steps #4 and #5 until the compass reaches the south pole of the magnet.
7. Observe the pattern of the plotted dots.

FIG 1

What Happened?

The plotted dots form a curved pattern from one end of the magnet to the other. This is because the magnetic needle of the compass lined up with the invisible magnetic field around the magnet. The south pole of the compass needle was attracted to the magnetic south pole of the magnet. The magnetic field lines curve in an arc around the magnet. Thus, the compass needle changes direction as it moves from the magnet's north pole to its south pole.

71. Temporary vs. Permanent Magnets

Some magnetic materials retain their magnetism when removed from a magnetic field. These are called **hard magnetic materials** and can become a **permanent magnet**, meaning the material retains its magnetism. Permanent magnets are made of materials such as alnico (an aluminum, nickel, and cobalt alloy) and ferrites (a mix of iron oxides with nickel, strontium, or cobalt). Permanent magnets have a high **coercivity**, which is the resistance of a magnetic material to changes in magnetization.

Soft magnetic materials gradually lose their magnetism when removed from the magnetic field, some faster than others. Soft magnetic materials, such as iron, iron-silicon alloys, and nickel-iron alloys form temporary magnets. These magnets have a low coercivity.

See for Yourself

Materials
strong magnet
small metal paper clips
small iron tacks

What to Do
1. Touch one paper clip to either pole of a magnet.
2. Make a paper clip chain by touching one paper clip at a time to the last hanging clip as shown in Figure 1. Add as many paper clips as possible.

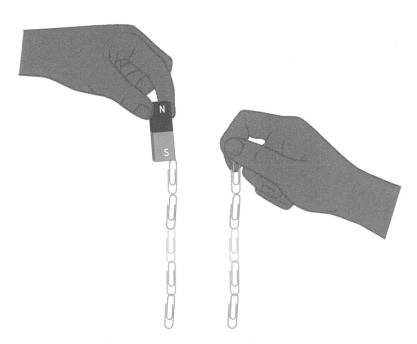

FIG 1   **FIG 2**

3. Carefully, so as not to shake the paper clip chain, remove the paper clip attached to the magnet.

4. Repeat steps #1 through #3 replacing the paper clips with the iron tacks.

What Happened?

When an unmagnetized magnetic material, such as paper clips and iron tacks used in this activity touch or are even brought near a magnet, they become a magnet themself. The materials are magnetized by a process called **magnetic induction**. The paper clips and iron tacks are soft magnetic materials, thus they become temporary magnets.

255

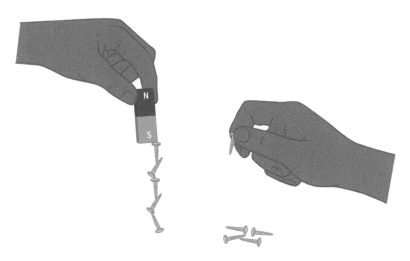

FIG 3

This means the magnetic domains in the materials lined up with the magnetic field of the magnet. Each link in the paper clip and tack chain was magnetized by the link with which they last made contact. When the paper clip chain was removed from the magnet, the paper clips remained together because they were temporarily magnetized. Being made of soft magnetic material, the paper clips will gradually lose their magnetism, meaning their domains will be randomly arranged.

The chain of iron tacks also was temporarily magnetized, but unlike the paper clips, the chain of tacks immediately fell apart. The tacks may have retained some magnetism, but not enough to overcome the pull of gravity.

256

72. Magnetic Permeability

Magnetic permeability means a material does not allow the magnetic field of a magnet to pass through. Instead, the magnetic force lines are gathered in by magnetically permeable materials. Therefore, only magnetic materials are permeable. Think of it as a shield taking in the magnetic field and not allowing it to go any further.

Nonmagnetic materials allow the magnetic force field of a magnet to pass through, thus they are **nonpermeable**. Magnets are often used to hold papers to metal cabinets and refrigerators. This is possible because paper is nonpermeable. Simply stated, the paper has no effect on the magnetic field of the magnet.

See for Yourself

Materials
bar magnet
book
metal paper clip
spatula with a metal blade

Note: Make sure the spatula blade is magnetic, so it is attracted to a magnet.

What to Do
1. Position the magnet so that its south pole is under one page of the book and the north pole is extending out.
2. Place the paper clip on top of the page over the magnet.

3. Hold the uncovered north end of the magnet and move the magnet around (Figure 1).

FIG 1

4. Observe the motion of the paper clip as the magnet moves.
5. Remove the magnet and replace it with the metal spatula.
6. Place the magnet under 3 or 4 pages beneath the spatula in the book.
7. Repeat steps #2 and #3 (Figure 2).

FIG 2

258

What Happened?

The paper is not attracted to the magnet, but the paper clip is. Moving the magnet caused the paper clip to move. Around every magnet is an invisible magnetic field. Some materials, such as paper, do not stop or disrupt the pattern of the field. Materials that allow a magnetic field to pass through without any disruptions in the magnetic field are said to be nonpermeable. Materials that do not allow the magnetic field to pass through, but instead seem to absorb the magnetic field are said to be magnetically permeable. Nonpermeable materials are not attracted to a magnet, unlike permeable materials that are attracted to a magnet. The magnetic field passes through the paper with no change in the direction of the field; thus, paper is nonpermeable. The metal spatula is magnetic. The spatula is permeable. When placed between the paper clip and the magnet, the magnetic field does not pass through the spatula. Instead, the magnetic field moves within the metal blade of the spatula, thus the magnetic force of the magnet no longer affects the paper clip.

73. Compass Rose

A **compass rose** is a drawing used to show directions on a map or a compass. It indicates the **cardinal directions** north (N), south (S), east (E), and west (W). Cardinal directions of north is also called **True North**. Cardinal directions line up with the Geographic North Pole. A compass rose, such as the one prepared in this activity, also has northeast (NE), southeast (SE), southwest (SW), and northwest (NW) marked at halfway intervals between cardinal directions.

See for Yourself

Materials
sheet of white plain paper
ruler
marking pen

What to Do
1. Fold the paper in half twice, first vertically from top to bottom, and then horizontally from side to side.
2. Open the paper and use the ruler and pen to draw two 7 inch (17.5 cm) lines on the fold lines. These lines need to be centered on the page.
3. Draw two diagonal 6 inch (15 cm) lines as shown in Figure 1.
4. Place an arrow head on the end of each of the lines and label the lines as in Figure 1.
5. Can you use the compass rose you prepared to determine actual directions? Keep the compass rose for Activity #74 Floating Compass.

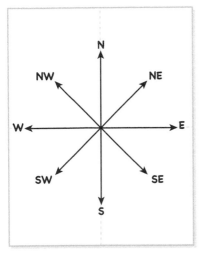

What Happened?

Have you ever looked through the glass cover of a compass? Underneath the needle you will see a compass rose! A compass rose that is printed on paper cannot be used alone to determine directions. A compass rose is often used with a compass. A compass has a freely rotating magnetic needle that always points to Earth's Magnetic North Pole. The compass rose helps to read the compass. Maps are drawn so that the north on the compass rose is **True North**, a direction pointing toward the Geographic North Pole. Sailors and pilots know that the needle on a compass responds to the Earth's magnetic field. Therefore, north as indicated on the compass rose around a compass does not direct one to True North, but rather it is toward Earth's **Magnetic North**.

74. Floating Compass

A compass is a simple device for determining cardinal directions, north, south, east, and west. It works by means of a freely rotating magnetized needle that aligns with Earth's Magnetic North and South Poles. Surprisingly, these magnetic poles are near, but not aligned with, Earth's Geographic North and South Poles, as determined by the Earth's axis. Instead, Earth's Magnetic Poles are produced by Earth's outer core, made of molten iron. Earth's rotation about its axis causes the molten iron to spin. This motion causes the free electrons in the iron to move in one direction resulting in the production of an electric current. All electric currents produce a magnetic field perpendicular to the movement of the electric current. Thus, Earth's twirling iron core produces a magnetic field around Earth. If you suspend a bar magnet, its north end will point toward Earth's Magnetic North Pole. The north pole of a magnet can more correctly be called the north-seeking pole.

See for Yourself

Materials
small clear disposable plastic cup
tap water
stainless steel sewing needle
bar magnet
sheet of paper towel
pencil
compass rose from Activity #73 Compass Rose
helper

What to Do

1. Lay the needle on top of the magnet with its pointy end toward the magnet's north pole for 3 or more minutes. Remove the magnet from the workspace so it cannot affect the results.
2. Fill the cup about three-quarters full of water. Place the compass rose on a table. Dry the outside of the cup and place it on top of the center of the compass rose.
3. Tear off a roughly 1-inch (1.25-cm) square from the paper towel.
4. Put the needle on the paper and carefully place the paper on the surface of the water (Figure 1).

FIG 1

5. If the paper is still under the needle, use the pencil to gently push the paper down into the water leaving the needle to float on the water's surface.
6. Ask your helper to slightly lift the cup. Then, rotate the compass rose underneath so that the needle point and north on the compass rose are in line (Figure 2).

263

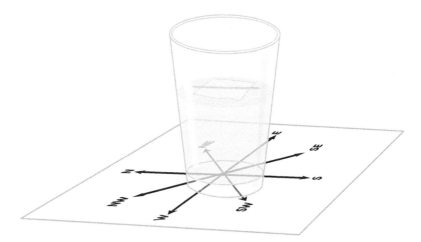

FIG 2

What Happened?

The paper and needle initially both float on the surface of the water. Then, the paper sinks, leaving only the needle on the water's surface. The needle is supported by the **surface tension** of the water, which acts like a thin skin. The water is able to form a surface skin due to the attraction of water molecules sticking to each other, called adhesion. In this way, the needle is still able to float freely and move in response to the force of the Earth's magnetic field. Thus, a magnetized floating needle becomes a compass that accurately points toward the Magnetic North and South Poles. The compass rose beneath the cup can be used to show other cardinal directions, just like it does inside the dome of a compass.

75. Magnetic Declination

Magnetic declination is the angle between True North, or Geographic North, and Geomagnetic North for a specific location. **True North** is the direction determined by the fixed end of Earth's axis, which we refer to as the North Pole. True North is the direction of sun shadows at solar noon, which is when the Sun is at its highest altitude in the sky. **Geomagnetic North** is the direction toward Earth's Magnetic North Pole. This is the location where the Earth's magnetic field goes vertically down into the planet. As shown in Figure 1, no matter where a person is on Earth, a compass directs them toward Magnetic North, which is not in the same location as True North. Compass directions are also called cardinal directions.

There is magnetic variation between a line pointed toward True North and a line pointed toward the Geomagnetic North Pole from a geographic location. Map directions are aligned with True North. Given the map coordinates of a location, travelers such as pilots or sailors need to know how to make adjustments when using a compass. An imaginary line connecting True North and Geomagnetic North is called the **agonic line.** A compass points toward the North Pole when the traveler is on the agonic line.

Magnetic Variation

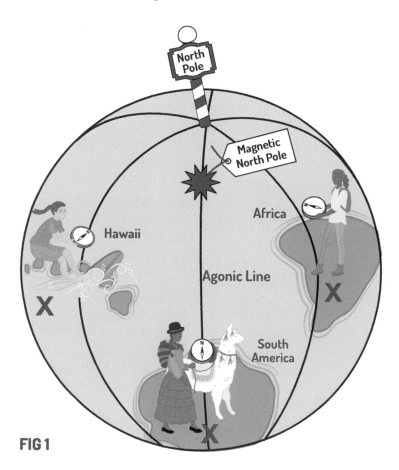

FIG 1

See for Yourself

Materials

pencil
sheet of cardstock or cardboard
2 metal brads
2 pieces of string, 8 inches (20 cm)

What to Do

1. Draw or trace around an outline of the USA on the card-stock. Using Figure 2, sketch the agonic line as shown.
2. At the top of the agonic line, use the pencil to make a hole in the paper. Insert one of the paper brads in the

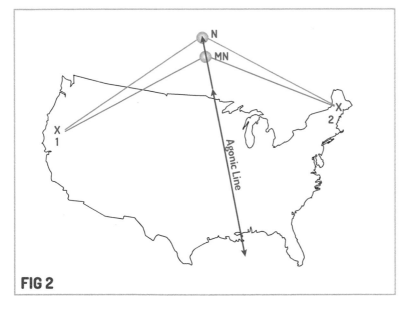

FIG 2

hole, and then tie the end of one of the strings to the brad. Label the brad, N, for the North Pole.

3. Repeat step #2, making a second hole on the agonic line about 1 inch (2.5 cm) from the brad that marks the North Pole. Label this brad, MN, for the Magnetic North Pole. Tie the second string to this brad.

4. Demonstrate the magnetic declination for different places on the map. Figure 2 gives two examples, one on the west coast and the other on the east coast of the USA.

5. For each location, you choose, place a dot on the map and pull the two strings together. Observe the angle formed by the strings.

What Happened?

There is no angle of declination if the location is on the agonic line. This is because the Magnetic North Pole and North Pole are in line with each other as shown in Figure 2. But, the angle of declination for a location increases the farther east or west of the agonic line a location is. The model in this activity will not give true angle measurement. They only represent how the angle forms. The location of the Magnetic North Pole continues to change. Since it was discovered in 1831, the Magnetic North Pole has moved about 1400 miles (2250 km). Thus, the angle of declination can be different from one year to the next. The Magnetic North Pole, in the year 2020, was at 80.65° N latitude and 72.68° W longitude.

76. Electromagnet

An electromagnet is a type of magnet produced by an electric current. When an electric current passes through a wire, a magnetic field is produced around the wire, but the strength of this magnetic field is very low and only present when the electric current is flowing. A stronger magnetic field can be generated by coiling the wire into a tightly packed cylinder of insulated wire. This cylindrical coil, called a **solenoid**, acts as a magnet when an electric current passes through the wire. An increase in the number of coils of wire will increase the magnetic strength of the solenoid. Also, inserting a soft magnetic rod, such as an iron nail, inside the core of the solenoid will increase the magnetic field. The iron nail becomes magnetized and adds to the overall strength of the magnetic field generated by the electromagnet. Soft magnetic materials, such as nails, paper clips, and iron tacks, only become magnetized temporarily when within a magnetic field. After being removed from the magnetic field, soft magnetic materials gradually lose their magnetism. Figure 1 shows an electromagnet being used to pick up vehicles and move them. After the electromagnet is disconnected from a supply of electric current, the magnetic field disappears and even though the temporary magnet used retains some magnetism, it is not enough to overcome the pull of gravity; thus, the car drops into the pile below.

FIG 1

270

See for Yourself

Materials

wire, 18-gage, insulated, 1 yard (1 m)
D cell battery
long iron nail
duct tape
rubber band
metal paper clips
wire stripper
adult helper

Caution: Disconnect the circuit as quickly as possible because the insulated wire and battery can get very hot.

What to Do

1. Holding the nail with the nail head on the left, bring the insulated wire up behind the nail (at the nail head end) and over the front. Continue winding the wire tightly around the nail, leaving about 6 inches (15 cm) of free wire on each end. You have made a solenoid with a soft iron core.

2. Using a wire stripper, have an adult helper strip about 1 inch (2.5 cm) of insulation off both ends of the wire.

3. Secure one end of the wire to the flat negative end of the battery with duct tape. Wrap the rubber band around the battery to press the wire tighter against the battery terminal.

4. Test the magnetic properties of the solenoid without a current by holding the battery in one hand and touching the nail tip to a pile of paper clips. Next, lift the nail and observe any paper clips clinging to the nail.

5. Hold the free insulated wire and touch its end to the battery. Repeat step #4

6. Remove the free end of the wire that you are holding against the battery terminal. Observe the effect on the paper clips.

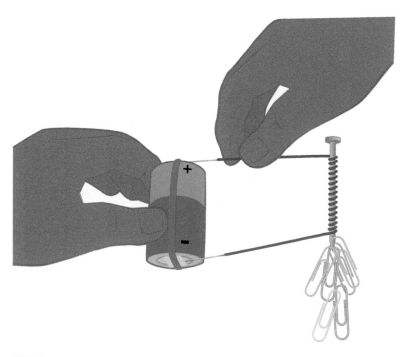

FIG 2

What Happened?

When the solenoid is connected to the battery, the paper clips stick to the tip of the iron nail. The electric current

272

flowing through the solenoid produces a magnetic field, which magnetizes the iron nail. We know this by the paper clips hanging on the nail. The iron nail becomes a temporary magnet that gradually loses its magnetism when removed from a magnetic field. Though the nail as well as the paper clips are temporarily magnetized, their magnetic strength is slowly decreasing. Some of the paper clips may fall as soon as the current stops, but some will continue to cling to the nail for a short time. Paper clips hanging from other paper clips fall because gravity is stronger than their magnetic attraction to each other.

77. Right-Hand Rule

The right-hand rule for a solenoid is used to determine the direction of the magnetic north pole of an electromagnet. The right-hand rule states that:

> *To determine the direction of the magnetic field for an electromagnet, start with the wire connected to the positive terminal of the battery and wrap the fingers of your right hand in the direction of the positive wire. Your thumb will point in the direction of the magnetic north pole of the electromagnet.*

From the positive pole through the solenoid, Figure 1 shows the same solenoid in both A and B. But the battery terminals have been switched. The polarity of an electromagnet depends on how the ends of a solenoid are connected to a battery. In this activity, you will use your right hand to determine the polarity of a solenoid if it were connected to a battery as shown in Figure 1.

A   B

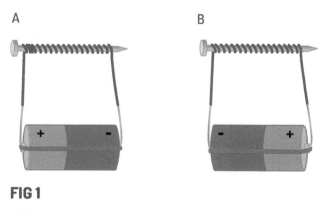

FIG 1

274

See for Yourself

Materials

solenoid from Activity #76 Electromagnet

What to Do

1. Hold the solenoid in your right hand with the pointy end of the nail pointing toward your thumb. Wrap your fingers up and over the coil of wire with your thumb and pointy end of the nail sticking out to the right as in Figure 2. Note your hand is wrapped in the direction the wire is wound if it had been wound coming from the positive battery terminal.

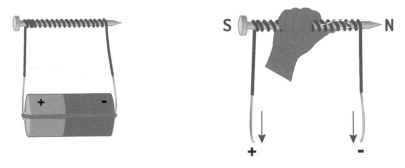

FIG 2

2. Again, hold the solenoid with your right hand, but this time place your hand over the solenoid. While holding the solenoid this time, your thumb will be pointing to the left as shown in Figure 3. Note that your right hand is wrapped in the direction the wire is wound if it had been wound coming from the positive battery terminal.

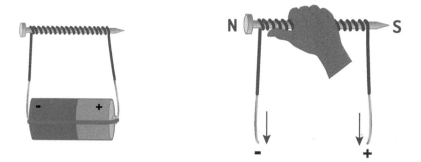

FIG 3

What Happened?

Using the right-hand rule, the direction of the north pole of the magnetic field produced by the solenoid shown in Figure 1A would be toward the pointed end of the nail. Turning the battery around, as in Figure 1B, also switches the polarity of the magnetic field. Thus, using the right-hand rule, the north pole of the magnetic field for Figure 1B would be toward the nail's head.

Although the solenoid used in this activity was not connected to a battery, you now know how to use the right-hand rule to determine the polarity of a magnetic field produced by an electromagnet.

276

78. Demagnetization

Demagnetize means to remove the magnetic field from a material. Only magnetic materials, which contain domains, can be magnetized. Domains are regions within the material in which the movement of some of the atom's electrons create a magnetic field. In a material that has been magnetized, the domains are lined up so that the magnetic north pole of each domain points in the same direction. Heating a magnet above a certain temperature, called the **Curie point**, will cause it to be demagnetized. Dropping a magnet also affects the alignment of its domains. Thus, dropping magnets can weaken their magnetic strength.

See for Yourself

Material
marker
10 toothpicks
small box, shoebox, or puzzle box

What to Do
1. Color one end of each toothpick with the marker; the toothpicks represent domains with the north pole colored.
2. Lay the toothpicks in the bottom of the box, which represents a magnet, so they are aligned with each other and the colored tips are pointing in the same direction as shown in Figure 1.

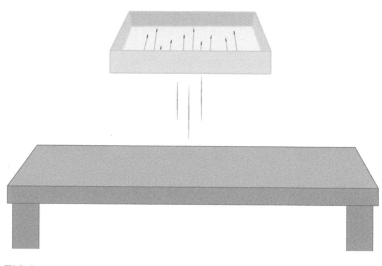

FIG 1

3. Lift the box about 1 foot (30 cm) above a tabletop.
4. Hold the box so that is it parallel with the tabletop and drop the box so that it lands on the table.
5. Observe the position and directions of the toothpicks after it hits the table.

What Happened?

The toothpicks are lined up to represent the domains in a magnet. Each colored tip represents the domain's north pole, and the poles are all pointing in the same direction. When the box is dropped, the kinetic energy of the box is transferred to the toothpicks, which move around and realign in a random pattern. This is an exaggerated representation of the realignment of domains in a magnet when dropped. Dropping a magnet one time may not totally demagnetize a permanent magnet, but it can reduce the strength of the magnet.

278

79. Dipping Needle

A device used to show the angle of the lines of a magnetic field around a magnet is a **dipping needle**. Basically, a compass held in a vertical position will act as a dipping needle. In the Northern Hemisphere, the north–seeking end of the dipping needle will dip down at an angle, depending on how near the device is to the Magnetic North Pole. At Earth's Equator, the dipping needle would be horizontal, but as one approached Earth's South Pole, the south end of the compass needle would dip down. A magnetized needle and a magnet can be used to model how a dipping needle works.

Interestingly, the author had the opportunity to prove this during her travels to Earth's Geographic South Pole. There, she personally experienced the change in Earth's magnetic field while watching the compass needle change angles. Since the Magnetic South Pole is not at the Geographic South Pole, the needle was never vertical, but very tilted. You will be able to witness this phenomenon without leaving your home in this activity!

See for Yourself

Materials
sewing thread, 1 foot (30 cm)
steel sewing needle, magnetic
cellophane tape
desk lamp
disk magnet

What to Do

1. Tie one end of the thread around the center of the needle.
2. Tie the free end of the thread to the desk lamp. Adjust the string so that the needle hangs 2 inches (5 cm) above the surface of the table.
3. Put a small piece of tape on one side of the magnet. Touch this side of the magnet to the point of the needle.
4. Move the magnet away from the needle and adjust the needle in the thread knot so that it hangs freely in a horizontal position as in Figure 1.

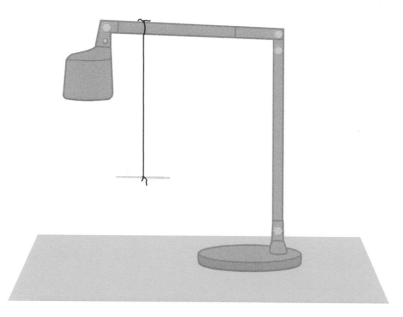

FIG 1

5. Set the magnet upright on its side and move it directly under the hanging needle. Next, find the position in

which the needle hangs horizontally when the edge of the magnet is under it.

6. Slowly tilt the magnet to the right and then to the left.
7. Observe the position of the needle as the magnet is tilted one way and then the other (Figure 2).

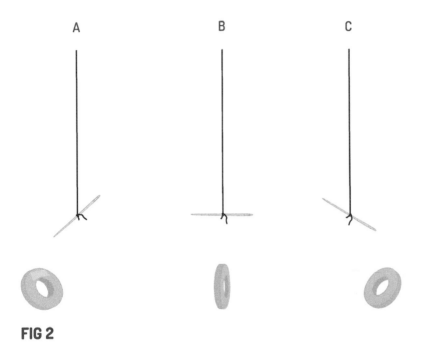

FIG 2

What Happened?

Before starting, touching the magnet with the needle magnetized it, and, like all magnets, the needle then had a north and south pole. The poles of disk magnets are on the flat faces. The magnetic field of the disk magnet circles the magnet from one side to the other. This magnetic field has the least dip, or angling above the edge of the magnet, thus the needle hangs horizontally when above this part of the magnet. On Earth, a dipping needle would not be tilted at the Equator, but as one moves toward one of Earth's Magnetic Poles, one end of the dipping needle tilts or dips down. While the north and south poles of the magnet were not identified, it was obvious by the movement of the dipping needle that the two sides or faces of the disk magnet were different.

The needle is relatively horizontal when suspended above the edge of the magnet, but as the magnet is tilted, the one end and then the other end of the needle dips or tips down toward the magnet. Figure 2A shows the pointed end of the needle dipping toward the side of the magnet marked with tape. Thus, the pointed end of the magnetic needle is attracted toward the magnet and the "eye" of the magnetic needle is being **repelled** by the magnet. Figure 2B shows the needle in a relatively horizontal position that changes in Figure 2C when the magnet is tilted, so that the marked side faces away from the needle.

80. Magnetic Energy

Energy causes change or motion. An object can have potential energy if two forces are acting on it in opposite directions. For example, in Figure 1, each pair of magnets are moved toward each other. Two forces acting on the magnets are the magnetic force repelling the magnets and the experimenter's hands are acting against this force. When the magnets are released, the magnetic potential energy of the magnets is converted to kinetic energy and the magnets move apart.

Magnetic Repulsion

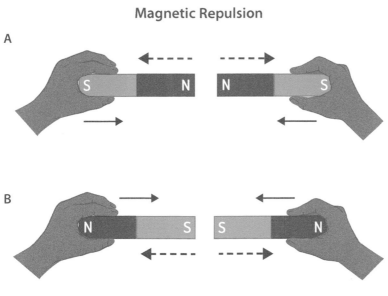

FIG 1

If unlike poles are near each other, they attract and move toward each other as shown in Figure 2. In this case, the magnetic force between the two magnets is pulling the magnets together. As long as the experimenter keeps the magnets close but not touching, they have magnetic potential energy. This potential energy is converted to kinetic energy when the magnets are released and they move toward each other.

Magnetic Attraction

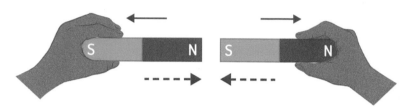

FIG 2

See for Yourself

Materials
2 disk magnets
tape
ruler

What to Do
1. Place a small piece of tape on one side of each of the magnets.
2. Place one of the magnets on a nonmagnetic table with the taped side facing up.
3. Stand a ruler next to the magnet and hold the second magnet, with its taped side facing up at the 4 inch (10 cm) mark on the ruler.

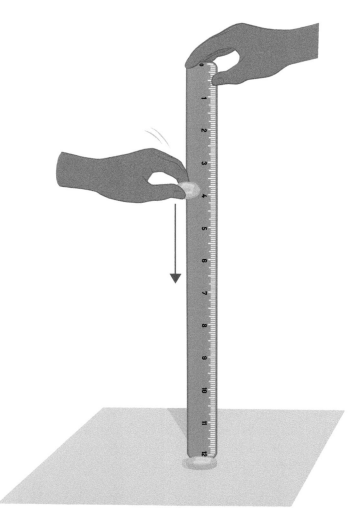

FIG 3

4. Slowly move the magnetic disk toward the magnet on the table (Figure 3).

285

5. Make a note of the distance between the two magnets when the lower magnet moves.

6. Repeat steps #2 through #5 with the taped side of the lower magnet facing down.

What Happened?

The taped sides of the magnets didn't mark magnetic poles. Instead, the tape was only a guide used to repeat the experiment with different sides of the magnets facing each other. When unlike poles of the two magnets were near, the magnetic potential energy of the lower magnet is converted into kinetic energy and it jumps up and sticks to the upper magnet. The distance between the two magnets before there is movement depends on the strength of the magnets. The stronger the magnetic force of attraction, the farther apart the magnets can be before their magnetic force causes motion. This magnetic attractive force has to be great enough to overcome the downward force of gravity acting on the magnet.

When the unlike poles of the two magnets were facing each other, the distance between them was very small before the bottom magnet moved to the side. Depending on the strength of the magnetic force of the magnets, you might be able to press the two magnets together, but you would feel the resistant force acting upward.

Glossary

Important terms are given in bold throughout the activities. Their definitions are presented here in alphabetical order.

absorption: Absorption means to take in.

acceleration: A change in velocity in a specific amount of time and specific direction. A net force causes acceleration; if the net force is gravity, the object will accelerate at a rate of 32 feet/second^2 (9.8 m/second^2) toward the center of Earth.

adhesion: Adhesion is the attraction between two dissimilar particles or surfaces, such as tape stuck on a surface.

agonic line: The agonic line is an imaginary line connecting True North and Geomagnetic North.

air pressure: Air pressure is a measurement of the force or weight of air pushing down on a specific surface area. The force of air above a 1 inch (2.5 cm) square area on Earth's surface at sea level is about 14.7 pounds (65.4 N).

air resistance: An example of fluid friction. Air resistance is the friction of air molecules on objects moving through air.

ampere, A: The unit for measuring an electric current. One ampere equals 1 coulomb per second; one coulomb equals 6.24 quintillion electrons.

amplitude: In reference to waves, amplitude is the height of the wave; the energy of a wave. In reference to sound, amplitude refers to loudness.

anode: The anode is the positive terminal; a positively charged electrode.

atom: The smallest building block of an element that retains the properties of the element; the atoms of an element all have the same number of protons.

attract: To be pulled together. Unlike charges attract or move toward each other.

balance: When the rotational torque on each side of a center of gravity is equal; it occurs when an object or system is supported at its center of gravity.

balanced forces: Forces acting on an object are balanced when the sum of these forces is zero; the net force equals zero.

balloon rocket: A rubber balloon filled with air that moves when propelled by pressure.

battery: A device that changes chemical energy into electrical energy. A battery has positive and negative terminals.

Bernoulli's principle: Bernoulli's principle states that an increase in the speed of fluid results in a decrease in pressure.

bob: A bob is the weight hanging on the end of a pendulum.

288

Bohr model: The Bohr atomic model looks much like a model of planets orbiting the Sun at different distances. Comparatively, in the Bohr model, negatively charged electrons orbit a positively charged nucleus in different energy levels.

bounce: Bounce is to rebound, or spring back, after hitting a surface.

cardinal directions: Cardinal directions refer to north (N), south (S), east (E), and west (W).

cathode: The negative terminal; a negatively charged electrode.

center of gravity: The location on an object where the weight of an object or system is considered to be concentrated; the point where the resultant force of gravity acts. If supported at this point, the object can be balanced.

charging by contact: Charging by contact occurs when an object with an excess or deficit number of electrons on its surface touches an uncharged object. Some of the excess electrons are transferred to or removed from the uncharged object.

circuit: *See* **electric circuit**.

closed circuit: In reference to electricity, a closed circuit is one with no breaks in its path.

Coandă effect: The Coandă effect is the tendency of a flowing fluid, either a liquid or a gas, to cling to a flat or convex surface in its path.

coercivity: Coercivity is a measure of resistance of a magnetic material to changes in magnetization.

compass rose: A compass rose, printed on a map or chart, indicates the cardinal directions north (N), south (S), east (E), and west (W).

compression: A type of stress that squeezes material together. The name of the compressed part of a longitudinal wave.

concave lens: A lens that is thinner in the center and thicker at its edge so it is curved inward; a diverging lens.

conductor: A material through which energy (heat or electricity) passes easily; metals are good conductors of both heat and electric current; have free electrons.

constructive interference: In reference to waves, constructive interference is when the waves that are in phase superpose, they overlap, trough to trough or from crest to crest.

converge: When things meet, they converge. Parallel light rays enter a convex lens and converge when exiting the lens.

convex lens: A lens that is thicker in the center than at its edges and is curved outward; a converging lens.

coupled pendulums: Coupled pendulums are two pendulums connected by some medium.

Curie point: Temperature at which a magnet can be demagnetized.

current: In reference to electricity, a current is the rate of electrons moving past a point; measured in amperes, (A). One ampere is equal to 6.24 quintillion electrons each second.

current electricity: A type of electricity related to the movement of electrons.

deceleration: A decrease in velocity over a specific time.

demagnetize: A magnet is demagnetized when its domains are randomly organized. This can occur if the magnet is heated or accidently dropped.

density: The measure of mass per volume; the quantity of matter in a specific volume.

destructive interference: In reference to waves, destructive interference is when two superposed (overlapping) waves are out of phase, or crest to trough.

dipping needle: A device used to show the angle of the lines of a magnetic field around a magnet.

diverge: When things separate or spread out, they diverge. Parallel light rays entering a concave lens diverge when exiting the lens.

drag force: The retarding force of fluids on objects moving through them; *also called* **fluid friction**.

dry cell battery: A dry cell battery is a type of electric battery. These batteries have one or more electrochemical cells, which can transform chemical energy into electrical energy.

Earth's acceleration of gravity: The force of attraction of things toward Earth's center; accelerates objects at a rate of 32 ft/s^2 (9.8 m/s^2) toward Earth's center.

eclipse: An eclipse is the blocking of the light by a body. In reference to celestial bodies, it is the blocking of light by one celestial body by the moving of another between it and the observer, or between it and its source of illumination.

effort arm: The side of a lever where the effort force is applied; *see* also **effort distance**, **effort force**.

effort distance: The length from the fulcrum of a lever to the effort force; *see* also **effort arm**, **effort force**.

effort force: The force you apply to one end of a simple machine; the force applied to a lever to move a load.

elastic potential energy: Elastic potential energy is a type of energy stored in an object that is stretched or compressed, such as a rubber band or spring.

electric circuit: The path that an electric current flows through; a loop of conductors forming the path.

electric current: An electric current is a flow of electric charges. The strength of the current is equal to the number of electric charges passing a given point per second. Electric current is measured in amperes.

electrical energy: Electricity is a form of energy produced by the movement of free electrons.

electricity: A form of energy associated with the presence and movement of electric charges; static electricity.

electrochemical energy: Electrochemical energy is stored chemical energy, such as in a battery; a type of potential energy that can be converted into electricity that can be converted into electrical energy.

electromagnet: An electromagnet is a type of magnet produced by an electric current.

electromagnetic: In reference to electromagnetic waves, consisting of both electric and magnetic fields.

electron: The negative particle found outside the nucleus of all atoms. Electrons move around the nucleus at different distances called energy levels.

electronegativity: The measure of how strongly electrons are attracted to the nucleus of an atom.

292

electroscope: An instrument that detects the presence of static charges.

electrostatic attraction: The attraction between two unlike charges.

electrostatic repulsion: The repulsion between like charges.

energy: The ability to do work; energy is used to do work. Types of energy include heat, light, and electricity, sound, chemical, mechanical, nuclear; types of energy: kinetic and potential.

energy level: Energy levels, or orbitals, of an atom are at fixed distances from the nucleus, with the electrons (e⁻) in each level having different amounts of energy.

equal-arm balance: An instrument used to compare the mass of an object.

ferromagnetism: Ferromagnetism is the unique ability of some materials, including iron, to exhibit magnetism.

filament: In reference to an incandescent light bulb, the filament is a thin wire that resists an electric current, causing it to get very hot and glow with a bright light. The electrical energy changes to heat energy and to light energy.

filter: In reference to light, a filter is a material that absorbs specific colors of light and allows other colors to pass through.

first-class lever: A first-class lever has the fulcrum (pivot point) between the load being lifted and the effort force needed to lift the load. A balance is a type of first-class lever.

fixed pulley: A fixed pulley stays in place; the pulley turns as the cord moves over the wheel, and a load is raised as the cord is pulled down.

flow rate: Flow rate is a measurement of the amount of material moving past a point each second.

fluid: A substance that has no particular shape and can flow; examples are a liquid or a gas.

fluid friction: The opposition to motion on objects moving through a fluid, such as air and water; *also called* **drag force**.

fluorescent: The property of a substance that can fluoresce; producing light when activated by high-energy light, such as ultraviolet light.

focal point: The focal point is where parallel light rays converge or, when these parallel rays diverge, it is the point where it appears diverging rays lead back to.

force: A push or pulling action on an object. *See also* **turning force**.

free electrons: Valence electrons in the atoms of materials with a low electronegativity. Free electrons are found in materials that conduct electricity as well as heat.

freefalling: To fall with Earth's gravity being the only downward force acting on the body.

frequency: Frequency is the number of times something happens in a specific amount of time. In reference to waves, it is the number of waves that pass a point in one second. In reference to vibrations, frequency is the number of back and forth movements in a specific amount of time. Frequency can be measured in **hertz** (**Hz**).

friction: A contact force that retards the motion of two surfaces moving against each other. *See also* **fluid friction, kinetic friction, rolling friction, sliding friction**, and **static friction**.

294

fulcrum: The point where a lever rotates, the pivot point.

Geomagnetic North: Geomagnetic North is the direction toward Earth's Magnetic North Pole.

gravitational field strength: The gravitational field strength near the surface of Earth is 9.8 N/kg. This means that for every 1 kg of mass an object has, Earth pulls on it with a force of 9.8 N.

gravitational potential energy: Energy an object has because it is raised above ground zero. In this position, the force of gravity can cause the object to accelerate toward the ground.

gravity: The force that attracts objects toward the center of Earth or toward any other body with mass; Earth's gravity accelerates objects at a rate of 32 ft/s^2 (9.8 m/s^2) toward the center of Earth.

ground state: The natural location of an atom's electrons.

hard magnetic material: Materials that retain their magnetism after being removed from a magnetic field. These materials form permanent magnets. See permanent magnets.

heat: The transfer of thermal energy; heat flows due to a difference in temperature from hot to cold.

hertz: Frequency is measured in hertz (Hz), where 1 Hz = 1 cycle per second or one back and forth vibration per second.

impulse: Impulse is the net force times the time required to stop a moving object. Impulse equals the change in momentum of the moving object.

incandescent light bulb: An incandescent light bulb produces light due to the heating of the filament in the bulb.

Incandescence is the emission of light due to being heated; examples include bonfires, some light bulbs, and the Sun as well as all other stars.

incident light: Light that strikes a surface.

inclined plane: A simple machine that has a tilted surface; it is used to move objects to a higher level.

inertia: The property of matter that resists any change in its state of motion unless acted on by a net force; if an object is moving it continues to move at a constant velocity unless acted on by a net force. Stationary objects remain stationary unless acted on by a net force.

in phase: In reference to waves, they are in phase when two crests and two troughs overlap.

insulator: A substance that resists, or limits, the movement of electric current as well as heat; examples are nonmetals, plastics, and air.

interference: Interference in physics means two waves superpose to form a resultant wave.

joule: An SI unit for work; a force of one newton moving an object a distance of one meter.

kinetic energy: The energy that an object has because it is in motion.

kinetic friction: The retarding force between an object and the surface it is moving across; also called sliding friction.

Law of Conservation of Energy: A law that states energy can neither be created nor destroyed, just transferred or changed into another form.

laws: Laws are descriptions, often mathematical, of natural phenomena believed to happen in the same way every time.

LED: A light-emitting diode is a device that does two things: gives off light and allows the current to flow in only one direction, which is from the positive lead of the LED through the circuit, back to the negative lead of the LED, through the LED, out the positive lead and the cycle starts over again.

lens: A transparent material, such as glass, with curved surfaces. A convex lens is thicker in the center than at the edges and a concave lens is thicker at the edges than in the center.

lever: A rigid bar with three parts: fulcrum, effort arm, and load arm; the bar rotates about the fulcrum (pivot point); force is applied to the effort arm; and the substance to be moved is on the load arm.

levitation: Levitation is the action of rising and being held aloft; suspended in the air without mechanical support.

lift: An upward force acting on an object; in reference to aircraft, the upward force on an aircraft due to the difference in the speed of air flowing over and under the wings.

light energy: Light energy is a form of wave energy and is a type of electromagnetic radiation (EMR or ER).

light transmission: Light transmission is the movement of light energy and its interaction with different mediums.

light waves: Light waves are transverse waves by which light energy is transmitted, but are not mechanical waves.

linear motion: Linear motion is motion in a straight line.

load: In reference to simple machine levers, the load is the object being moved.

load arm: The end of a lever supporting the load; where the load force is applied; *see also* **load distance**, **load force**.

load distance: The length from the fulcrum of a lever to the load force; *see also* **load arm**, **load force**.

load force: The force that a load applies to a lever.

longitudinal wave: A wave that has a back and forth motion; has areas of compression and rarefaction; sound waves are an example.

lunar eclipse: A lunar eclipse occurs when the Moon is full and moves into Earth's shadow.

machine: A device that makes work easier, faster, can change the direction of the force applied, or can increase or decrease the input force.

magnetic declination: Magnetic declination is the angle between True North, or Geographic North, and Geomagnetic North for a specific location; the angle between True North and cardinal north on a compass.

magnetic domains: Regions found only in magnetic material, such as iron, in which the magnetic properties of the atoms are aligned. These clusters of atoms behave like individual magnets with their magnetic poles lining up to point in the same direction.

magnetic field: The area around a magnet in which the magnetic force of the magnet affects the movement of other magnetic objects. Invisible lines of magnetic force coming out of the north pole and entering the south pole form the magnetic field around a magnet.

magnetic force: The force of attraction or repulsion between magnets, or between magnets and magnetic materials.

magnetic induction: Magnetic induction is the process by which an unmagnetized magnetic material, when touching

298

or brought close enough to be within the magnetic field of a magnet, becomes a magnet itself.

magnetic materials: Materials that have magnetic domains; they are attracted to a magnet and are ferromagnetic materials. Iron is one example.

Magnetic North: Magnetic North is the point on Earth's surface in the Northern Hemisphere where Earth's magnetic field points vertically downward; the north-seeking arrow of a compass points in this direction.

magnetic permeability: Magnetic permeability means a material allows the magnetic field of a magnet to enter but not to pass through, or exit. Instead, the magnetic field lines are gathered in by the material. Magnetic materials have a high magnetic permeability.

magnetic pole: On a magnet, there are two poles, north and south. If free to rotate, the north end of a bar magnet points toward Earth's Magnetic North Pole while the south end points toward Earth's Magnetic South Pole. On Earth, the Magnetic North Pole is a point in the Northern Hemisphere where Earth's magnetic field points vertically down, and the Magnetic South Pole is a point in the Southern Hemisphere where Earth's magnetic field points vertically upward.

magnetism: Magnetism is the magnetic force of attraction or repulsion between magnets, or between magnets and ferromagnetic materials.

mass, *m*: The amount of matter in an object.

massing pan: A massing pan is located on each end of an equal-arm balance. An object being compared is placed on the pan with objects or gram weights placed on the other pan to determine the mass of the object(s).

matter: Anything that takes up space and has mass. Matter, composed of atoms, is the stuff of which everything in the Universe is made.

mechanical advantage, MA: Mechanical advantage means that a machine multiplies the force applied, the effort force. A mechanical advantage greater than one indicates a ratio showing that the load force is greater than the effort force; thus, your effort force is being multiplied. The equation for mechanical advantage is: MA = load force/effort force.

mechanical energy: Mechanical energy is the sum total of an object's potential energy and kinetic energy.

mechanical waves: Waves that require a medium for transmission.

momentum: Momentum describes mass in motion and is a vector quantity. The equation is: momentum = mass × velocity.

moveable pulley: A moveable pulley is a machine that is able to move with the load that is being moved allowing for less force to be used to raise an object than if the object was lifted vertically without the pulley, or if a fixed pulley was used.

movement: Movement is the act of changing an object's physical location.

natural frequency: The frequency at which a material will vibrate if struck. The greater the mass of the material, the slower the vibrations, and vice versa.

negative terminal: In reference to a battery, a negative terminal is the part that maintains a negative charge.

net force, F_{net}: The resulting force after all other forces acting on an object have been considered. A net force has direction; it is a **resultant force**.

300

neutral atom: An atom with an equal number of protons and electrons. An atom with a net charge of zero.

neutrons: Particles found in the nucleus of an atom. This particle has no charge.

newton, N: A newton is the International Standard (SI) unit for force.

newton-meter: A force of one newton moves an object a distance of one meter.

Newton's First Law of Motion: This is the law of inertia; objects do not change their state of motion unless acted upon by an outside force. Objects at rest do not move unless acted upon by an outside force and objects in motion continue to move at a constant velocity unless acted upon by an outside force.

Newton's Second Law of Motion: A force acting on an object causes it to accelerate; the net force on an object is equal to the object's mass times its acceleration. The equation is $F = ma$.

Newton's Third Law of Motion: For every action, there is an equal and opposite reaction. When one object pushes on another, the second object pushes back with an equal force but in the opposite direction; the forces are acting on different objects.

nonpermeable: In reference to magnetism, a nonpermeable material allows a magnetic field to pass through it and exit the material. Nonmagnetic materials are generally classified as nonpermeable.

normal: In reference to ray diagrams, normal is a line perpendicular to a surface.

normal force: A normal force is a perpendicular force of one object acting on the surface of another object.

nucleus: The center of an atom where positively charged protons and neutrons with no charge (neutral) are located; the nucleus has an overall positive charge.

oblique: Oblique refers to being at an angle to a surface.

opaque: Characteristic of a substance or object that blocks visible light; it cannot be seen through. An object behind an opaque object cannot be seen.

open circuit: In reference to electricity, an open circuit is one with a break in its path that prevents the flow of electricity.

optical density: Optical density refers to the degree to which a material slows the speed of light that enters it. It depends on the length of time between light absorption by an atom and the light being re-emitted.

optical illusion: An optical illusion is a perception by the brain that doesn't match what is real.

out of phase: In reference to waves, out of phase is the superposition of the crest and trough of two waves.

pendulum: A pendulum is a weight suspended from a pivot point so that it can freely move back and forth. A tire swing is one example of a pendulum.

permanent magnets: A classification for magnets that retain their magnetism. Made of hard magnetic materials, such as alnico (an aluminum, nickel, and cobalt alloy) and ferrites (a mix of iron oxides with nickel, strontium, or cobalt)

photon: A bundle of light energy; particles which transmit light; released when an atom's excited electron returns to its ground state.

302

physics: The study of matter and energy and how they interact; the study of how forces affect the motion of objects.

pitch: The highness or lowness of a sound is called its pitch. Pitch is determined by the frequency of a sound, the lower the frequency, the lower the sound, and vice versa. In reference to a screw, the pitch is the number of spiral ridges or threads in one inch (2.5 cm). The smaller the pitch, the greater the mechanical advantage, meaning it is easier to turn the screw.

pivot point: The point about which an object rotates; the balancing point of a seesaw; the center of a merry-go-round; and the fulcrum of a lever.

plano-convex lens: A lens that is flat on one side and curved outward on the opposite side.

plumb bob: An instrument used to determine a vertical line; a weight hanging on a string.

polarization: In reference to light, polarization is the process of separating light waves moving in different planes. In reference to charges, it is the separation of positive and negative charges. In reference to atomic particles, such as atoms or molecules, it means to separate their positive and negative charges.

polarized lens: A lens designed to allow light rays moving only in one plane to pass through it.

polarized light: Light waves vibrating in one plane.

positive terminal: In reference to a battery, the positive terminal is the part that maintains a positive charge.

potential electrical energy: Potential electrical energy is potential energy due to the build up of electric charges.

potential energy: The energy of an object due to its position, such as being raised above the ground or being stretched; stored energy, such as energy in chemical bonds; examples are the energy in a compressed spring and the energy of a car at the top of a ramp.

pressure: Pressure is a measurement of force on an area; pressure is measured in pounds per square inch, psi (pascals, Pa, or newtons per square meter). *See* **air pressure**.

pressure wave: Pressure wave is another name for sound wave because sound waves increase and decrease in pressure as they move through a medium. This wave contains an area of increased pressure, called compression, and an area of decreased pressure, called rarefaction.

principal axis: In reference to lenses, the principal or primary axis is a straight line going through the center of a lens.

protons: Positively charged particles in the nucleus of an atom.

pulley: A simple machine that consists of a wheel, usually grooved, that holds a cord and is used to lift or lower an object.

radiation: Electromagnetic energy; wave energy that can travel through space; light energy; seven types of light radiation listed from the greatest energy having the highest frequency and shortest wavelength to the least energy with the lowest frequency and longest wavelength are gamma rays, X-rays, ultraviolet light, visible light, infrared light, microwaves, and radiowaves.

rarefaction: The name of the expansion of a longitudinal wave; area of decreased pressure.

ray diagrams: Ray diagrams are drawings that represent the paths of light rays.

real image: Real images occur where light rays converge and can be projected on a screen.

reed: A thin strip of material that vibrates to produce sound; part of some wind instruments.

reflect: Reflect means to bounce back off of a surface.

refract: Refraction is the bending, or changing direction, of light rays due to a change in speed as they enter a medium with a different optical density.

refractive index: A reference to the speed of light in a medium. It is the ratio of the speed of light in a vacuum to the speed of light in a medium.

repel: To push or move away due to a force. Like charges repel or move away from each other.

resultant force: The resultant force is the sum of all the forces acting on every part of an object.

right-handed screw: A screw designed to be turned clockwise, toward the right.

right-hand rule: The right-hand rule determines the direction for the magnetic field of an electromagnet. This rule states that: To determine the direction of the magnetic field for an electromagnet, start with the wire connected to the positive terminal of the battery and wrap the fingers of your right hand in the direction of the positive wire. Your thumb will point in the direction of the magnetic north pole of the electromagnet.

rolling friction: The resistance to the motion of rolling objects over a surface.

rotation: The turning of an object about its own axis; turning around a fixed point called a pivot.

rotational inertia: Rotational inertia is a measure that represents how difficult it is to start or stop the rotation of an object. Rotational inertia depends on the mass of the object and how this mass is distributed. The farther the mass is from the axis of rotation, the higher the rotational inertia.

rotational kinetic energy: Rotational kinetic energy is the energy of an object moving about an axis or pivot point.

screw: A screw is an inclined plane wrapped around a cylinder.

second-class lever: A simple machine that has the load between the fulcrum and the effort force; the mechanical advantage can be calculated using this equation: MA = effort distance/load distance

shadow: A dark shape produced when an object blocks a light source.

simple machine: The simplest device used to change the direction or magnitude of a force that is used to do work; examples include levers, pulleys, and wedges.

sliding friction: This is the resistance of motion between two surfaces moving against each other. *Also called* **kinetic friction**.

slope: A slope is a measure of how steep a slanted surface is.

soft magnetic materials: A class of materials that gradually lose their magnetism when removed from a magnetic field, some faster than others. Materials such as iron, iron-silicon alloys, and nickel-iron alloys are examples that form temporary magnets.

solenoid: A solenoid is a cylindrical coil of wire that acts as a magnet when an electric current passes through it.

sound: A sensation perceived by an organism's sense of hearing produced by the stimulation of hearing organs by sound waves.

sound energy: Sound energy is a type of energy produced by vibrating objects. This type of energy is transferred through a medium, such as a solid, liquid, or a gas. Sound energy is a form of energy that can be heard by living organisms.

sound transmission: The movement of sound energy via longitudinal waves.

sound waves: A type of energy produced by vibrations that travel through a medium in the form of longitudinal waves.

spectrum: The colors of light that, when mixed, form white light; when separated by a prism they are in order: red, orange, yellow, green, blue, indigo and violet.

spiral ridge: A spiral ridge is the raised ledge on a screw; also called a thread or spiral edge.

static electricity: A collection of electric charges in one place.

static friction: A "gripping" type of friction between stationary objects and the surface they are sitting on.

superpose: In reference to waves, superpose means to overlap.

surface tension: A skin-like surface across liquids due to the electrostatic attraction between the molecules of the liquid; water has strong surface tension.

system: A combination of objects working as a unit.

temperature: The measure of warmth or coldness caused by the average kinetic energy of vibrating particles in a material.

temporary magnets: A temporary magnet is made of soft magnetic materials that gradually lose their magnetism after being removed from a magnetic field.

terminal: In reference to a battery, it is one of the ends where an electric circuit is attached.

terminal velocity: The final velocity reached by a falling object when the two forces acting on it, drag force and gravity, are equal; thus, the net force is zero and the object is no longer accelerating.

thermal energy: Thermal energy is also known as heat energy.

third-class lever: A lever with the effort force between the fulcrum and the load. A shovel, a fishing rod, and tweezers are examples of a third-class-lever.

thrust: Thrust is a propulsive force; it is a forward force.

torque: A turning force that causes an object to rotate around a pivot point; torque = force × distance to the pivot point.

translational kinetic energy: Translational kinetic energy is the energy of an object moving in a straight line.

translucent: A material that allows some light to pass through, but changes the direction of the light. Materials behind a translucent material cannot be seen clearly.

transparent: A material that allows light to pass straight through. Objects behind a transparent material can be seen clearly.

transverse wave: Waves that move up and down like water waves, and have a crest and trough.

triboelectric effect: The triboelectric effect is a method of producing static electricity. This method requires the materials to be in contact with each other and then separated.

True North: A direction pointing toward the Geographic North Pole; direction of a sun shadow at solar noon in the Northern Hemisphere.

turning force: Torque, which is the force applied times the distance to the center of the object being rotated.

unbalanced force: An unbalanced force is a net force; it is a **resultant force**, meaning it is the sum of all the forces.

unpolarized light: Light that consists of light waves that vibrate. Each individual light wave vibrates in just one plane; however, there are multiple light waves traveling together, each vibrating in their own plane.

valence electrons: Electrons generally found in the outermost energy level of an atom.

velocity: The speed of a moving object in a specific direction.

vibrate: Vibrate means move back and forth.

vibrational kinetic energy: Vibrational kinetic energy is the energy caused by a back and forth movement.

virtual image: In reference to concave lenses, virtual images occur at the point where diverging lights rays appear to come from and cannot be projected on a screen.

wave: A wave is a transfer of energy without transporting the material; a disturbance that moves through a medium without transporting the medium.

wavelength: The distance between one wave and the next; the wavelength for water waves is the distance from crest to crest or from trough to trough.

wedge: A wedge is a simple machine shaped like an inclined plane; it is a moveable inclined plane.

weight, F_{wt}: The sum of all the forces of gravity acting on every part of an object; weight is the resultant force of gravity.

wheel and axle: A simple machine made up of an axle attached to a wheel.

white light: White light is produced by the combination of all the visible light energy in the electromagnetic spectrum.

wind: The movement of air masses in a horizontal direction to Earth's surface from an area of high air pressure to an area of lower air pressure.

work: Accomplished when a force is applied to an object and the object moves.

Index

312

313